Praise for
The Joy of Losing Your Job

"The JOY of Losing Your Job is an invaluable testament to the fact that difficult situations can yield profound opportunities, and that our biggest challenges open the door to unexpected personal and professional growth."

Michelle Tillis Lederman, Author of *The 11 Laws of Likability* and *Nail the Interview, Land the Job*

"Christina's story, and those of the people in this book, certainly show how even the most stressful circumstances can lead to amazing transformations and newly found focus. These moving stories of those who've "been there" and thrived will surely inspire the newly unemployed."

Bruce D. Schneider, Founder, Institute for Professional Excellence in Coaching (iPEC)

"Joblessness can be frightening, alienating and emotionally draining. It can also be a blessing in disguise. This is why the content and timeliness of this book is so helpful. Thank you, Christina DeOliveira, for inviting me to share one of my own life-changing stories of job loss in this book. Hopefully, it will inspire and touch the lives of all who read it. If you are in transition, read this book: *The JOY of Losing Your Job...HOPE Beyond Blood, Sweat and Tears."*

John J. Murphy, Award-Winning Author and Transformational Leader

"This book, and the inspiring stories of the people within it, demonstrates what can become of painful and uncertain situations when we look deep inside ourselves. Christina has done a wonderful job capturing that success is possible even when hope, faith, determination and dreams are temporarily dismantled from job loss."

Robert D. Micera, Corporate Leader, Educator and Author of *Right To The Point, The RDM Employer of Choice Model: Creating a Great Work Environment*

"Christina harnesses the power of personal stories to focus on how, in the midst of loss, we can find joy and abundance. Written with passion, faith and hope the message of her book is a message that needs to be heard–stories of ordinary people facing extraordinary difficulties and experiencing resilience and renewal. In this age of 'disruptable work,' many of us will be disrupted; this book shows us how others have turned that experience to their advantage, to joy and built an abundant and purposeful life out of a situation fraught with disappointment and fear. Christina's book is something we all need to read now, before we get disrupted!"

Kevin P. Shields, Vice President, ADP Field Initiatives

THE JOY
OF LOSING
YOUR JOB

CHRISTINA DEOLIVEIRA, MBA, CPC, ELI-MP

The JOY of Losing Your Job
Hope Beyond Blood, Sweat and Tears
By Christina DeOliveira, MBA, CPC, ELI-MP
Coche Press

Published by Coche Press, West Orange, New Jersey
Copyright ©2016 Christina DeOliveira
All rights reserved

Printed in the United States of America

Editor: Meeghan Truelove
Front cover design: Fred Pesce, Vertigo Media Group, www.VertigoMediaGrp.com
Back cover design: Yvonne Parks, www.PearCreative.com
Interior design and layout: Yvonne Parks, www.PearCreative.com
Cover copy: Lisa Canfield, www.copycoachlisa.com
Author photography: Mahvash Saba, Saba Photography, www.headshotsaba.com

ISBN: 978-0-9971325-0-2
Library of Congress Control Number: 2015920645

DEDICATION

With all my love and affection, this book is dedicated to:

David DeOliveira. You were my brother and best friend. Now you're my guardian angel and guiding light, illuminating my path in life. Thank you for being part of my journey, then and now—it would be meaningless without you.

My parents. Thank you for your unwavering love and support and for never giving up on me, even when I wanted to give up on myself. Your love has made me who I am and I love you both unconditionally.

My children, Michael and Monica. You are the light of my life and you will not understand just how much I adore you until you have children of your own. You are my world, my everything, and the reason I'm able to share these inspirational stories with those who need them most.

DONATION

All proceeds from the sale of this book are being donated to:
David's Gift Scholarship Foundation

David's Gift Scholarship Foundation was founded in February 2015, in memory of beloved coach, teacher, husband, son and brother David DeOliveira, who tragically succumbed to brain cancer in 2011. It is an academic foundation dedicated to helping deserving high school seniors with financial needs from East Side High School in Newark, New Jersey, by providing them with scholarships to continue their educations beyond high school. The intention is to help these deserving scholars achieve their career goals, an objective with the added benefit of bettering the community at large.

For information go to: www.davids-gift.org

CONTENTS

PREFACE

If you're reading this book, chances are you've lost your job or know someone (or several people) who have. If so, I want you to know that I have written and compiled this book for you. Yes, you!

Losing a job, especially one that was a huge part of your life, is not easy. In fact, some say it's comparable to something as tragic as losing a loved one. Perhaps not for everyone, but for far too many people, that's exactly what it's like.

Losing a job can be challenging for a number of reasons: Our identities are often wrapped up in our work, our financial situations may be precarious, responsibility for our families can weigh heavily on our shoulders and we may be steeped in fears about our future. We may have also felt deeply connected to our coworkers and the social life that revolved around work.

So losing your job can provoke a profound sense of loss. It's an emotional roller coaster that runs the gamut from sadness and anger to feelings of rejection and betrayal, often layered with a lost sense of purpose and direction. And during a time when people need to stay as flexible and positive as possible, many go rigid with fear and veer into a downward spiral of despair for a very long time.

It sucks!

The U.S. Bureau of Labor Statistics recently reported that the number of unemployed persons in this country is 7.9 million. Of those, 2.1 million are long-term unemployed (jobless for 27 weeks or more). Yet even with so many people in this same situation, when it happens to us we still can't help but feel alone, lost and confused by our circumstances. What just happened? How did I get here? And what the hell am I going to do now?

Well, my friends, I am here to tell you that you are not alone. During my own journey with job loss, I had the good fortune to meet several people who had been in my same situation and faced many of the fears and challenges I faced. The majority of these people were happy and fulfilled, and they all said the same thing: "Losing my job was the best thing that happened to me."

I listened to these people and I took note of their advice, and soon found myself saying the same thing. Not right away, of course— it took a while. But the day came when I realized that the person I had become and the things I was now doing with my life could not have been possible without those job-loss experiences.

This book is not a how-to for landing a new job. You will not find interviewing techniques or résumé-writing skills here. This is a compilation of stories from real people, just like you and me, who have experienced job loss and not only survived but thrived, growing happier and more fulfilled than they ever thought they could be. They shared their stories because they all in their own ways want to pass along the message that there is life after job loss, and it can be better than ever.

Throughout their journeys, as well as my own, a number of lessons about the experience of job loss were distilled. I've arranged the stories in this book using those lessons as a guide, grouping the stories by some of the biggest takeaways that can be learned from each of them.

I must acknowledge the bravery that came with sharing these stories and the willingness to "show up and be seen with no guarantee of outcome"—the definition of being vulnerable, according to author Brené Brown in her latest book, *Rising Strong*. Our personal and professional lives are intrinsically intertwined, and while we would like to think we can keep them separate and that one does not affect the other, there is nothing farther from the truth. They are one, and as such when we experience bumps in our personal lives they impact our professional lives, and vice versa. You will recognize this connection throughout many of the stories shared in this book. The beauty in owning our stories of struggle and sharing them with others is that we can write our own endings. And that, my friends, is exactly what the brave, wonderful storytellers in this book have done or are in the process of doing—writing their own happy endings.

About hope. What is hope, and why is it so important? Well, no one puts it better than Brené. She writes, "I've found that moving out of powerlessness, and even despair, requires hope. Hope is not an emotion. It's a cognitive process—a thought process made up of what researcher C.R. Snyder called the trilogy of 'goals, pathways and agency.' Hope happens when we can set goals, have the tenacity and perseverance to pursue those goals, and believe in our own abilities to act." I love this explanation—I hope you do, too.

Now, famous comedian Jim Carrey may disagree with Brené, C.R., and me. In his inspirational video, a commencement address at the 2014 Maharishi University of Management graduation, he says, "I don't believe in hope. Hope is a beggar. Hope walks through the fire and faith leaps over it." In Jim's defense, I also have to share what he said just before making this statement: "Let's take a chance on faith, not religion, but faith, not hope, but faith."

I get it, Jim. I do believe in the power of faith, but as I am sure that you know if you are reading this book, there are times when life can hit us hard, the rug gets pulled out from under us again and again, and we lose faith, hope and any sense of meaning or purpose in life. It can feel like existing in a big black hole.

Thankfully, many of us get beyond those dreadful, dark days. But getting to that point sometimes takes baby steps, and it could take quite some time to regain a sense of faith. Before getting to faith, we might choose hope: hope that things can one day be better, hope that we can find our way again, hope that we can be awakened to what the life lessons are trying to teach us. So, you see, for me—and I believe for many others—hope can be a stepping stone to faith.

My wish for you, my dear readers, is that the stories in this book will fill you with a sense of hope, and give you a stepping stone that leads to faith, wherever you are in your life. I wish for you to understand that you, too, will get through this difficult time. In fact, you will be better, stronger, wiser, happier and more fulfilled for it. And one day you will say, "Losing my job was the best thing that could have happened to me."

REPEAT AFTER ME: "My current situation is not my final destination."

Now, let's dive in!

A SPECIAL NOTE:

If you are currently in transition, or know someone who is, and in the process of writing a happy ending, we would LOVE to hear your story. Please share it on <u>www.performancecontinuum.com</u> and it may be included in a future edition of this book.

INTRODUCTION
INNER AWAKENING

"Sometimes, the bad things that happen in our lives put us directly on the path to the best things that will ever happen to us." —Nicole Reed

It was a Saturday morning in 1983 and I was 15 years old, a sophomore in high school. My parents, brother and I drove to Newark, as we did almost every weekend, to pick up imported goodies from our parents' home country of Portugal and have lunch at our favorite café. As we drove in, I looked up at the white Prudential building—the one that's so visible as you're landing at Newark Airport—as I did every time we made this trip. I announced to my family: "I'm going to work there one day."

I didn't know how I would be working there, or what I would be doing. Truth is, at that stage I didn't even know what Prudential was. All I knew was that I would work there one day.

Fast-forward four years, an associate's degree later, when I was hired by Prudential for my first real job out of school as a marketing coordinator. It was 1987, I was 19 years old and I was the only female in a predominantly male environment. Needless to say, it was not easy to be taken seriously. There were those in my department who said I'd never last more than a year.

But I did last more than a year. In fact, I lasted 24 years! And throughout those years I enjoyed a progressive, award-winning career in a variety of exciting and challenging roles that allowed me to develop into the professional I knew in my heart at the age of 15 that I could someday be.

During my years at Prudential, I took full advantage of their tuition assistance program. I finished my Bachelor of Science in Business Administration (BSBA) and earned several professional certifications, securities licenses and a master's certificate in Advanced Project Management from Villanova University. Finally, I earned my MBA in Global Entrepreneurship and Business Administration. I did this all through night school while working full time, being married and, eventually, raising two kids. And it was all possible thanks to Prudential, a generous company.

As I started to have children, the company afforded me something that was unheard of at that time in the early 1990s: work-life balance via telecommuting. My husband was an international airline pilot and was away quite a bit. I used to joke that I was a single mother most of the time, because, truthfully, that's how it felt. I needed workplace flexibility in order to be there for my kids and was fortunate to report to a woman who would become one of my greatest mentors and role models. She encouraged me to telecommute when I needed to. She would say to me, "I trust you, and why should I care where you're doing your work from as long as you're getting the job done?"

That may not seem like much today, but back then that was some seriously progressive action on her part. She never made me feel guilty and was fully supportive and compassionate about my situation. When anyone questioned it, she defended our agreement and stood by it. The demanding logistics of my life were made so much easier because I had this extraordinary, forward-thinking woman in my court. It was yet one more example to me of how servicing others to do their best work is a powerful, life-altering approach that I want to champion. But more on that later...

It's true that there were plenty of "corporatocities" at Prudential, but that is the case in every large organization. Prudential supported my growth and development, compensated me well for the work I did, respected my need for work-life balance and so much more. So what more could I ask for, right?

Well, in 2001, life hit me hard. My baby brother and only sibling, David, was diagnosed with a brain tumor. He was only 28 years old. My first response was, "No way! A brain tumor? Cancer? There's no history of cancer in our family, so how can this be? It must be a mistake."

For the next three weeks David suffered seizure after seizure, because the tumor was so large it was touching his motor strip. David said he would rather die than live with these seizures, so the decision was made to remove it. I found the best neurosurgeon possible, thankfully right in our backyard in New York City. Surgery was scheduled, and our gifted surgeon, Dr. Jeffrey Bruce of New York Presbyterian Hospital, removed 100 percent of the tumor. Not two weeks later, my brother was back at work, teaching and coaching girls' volleyball at Newark's East Side High School, a job he loved so much. "My kids need me," he said.

The biopsy from his tumor came back: an anaplastic astrocytoma, stage 3. Not good news. The diagnosis was that at best he would have three to five years to live. My response: No, sir! I was not going to lose my brother that soon.

Although he was five years younger, David had always been more like a big brother to me. He was protective, watched out for me and was always there when I needed him. There was no way I could live my life without him in it. I prayed harder than I ever prayed for anything in my life. We all did—our family, his students and friends, our whole extended community. And our prayers were answered, for a while.

Not long after I went through the hell of my brother's situation, something started to fester inside me. A new dream, a new ideal for my life. My vision wasn't clear yet, but for some reason it was becoming undeniable that I had fallen out of love with my once dream job at that wonderful company.

I put those feelings aside, focusing on being thankful for what was good in my life, and the fact that my job allowed me to meet my personal obligations and to provide a comfortable life for my kids and my family. I satisfied the hunger that was growing inside my heart by getting involved in volunteer work. I took leadership roles in the local Girl Scouts, a high school marching band, a missionary project to build a school in Haiti and more. I even started my own side business with two partners: Catering Angels. We loved to cook, bake and share our talents, but after a while it turned into way more work than it was worth, and it just wasn't fun anymore. I had dipped my toes in that "something else" work pool, but eventually we mutually agreed to dissolve the company.

Then, in 2007, life's next big blow hit. It was October 1, and I had just completed a walkathon fundraiser in support of my father-in-law, who had Alzheimer's disease. I caught the flu and was home from work, sicker than a dog—fever, chills, sore throat, the works. My husband of 18 years came home from a trip and promptly informed me that we were getting divorced. I was completely blindsided. He did not let me speak, there was no discussion, his mind was already made up and he was on the verge of calling my parents, who were in Portugal at the time, just three weeks from coming home. I was in shock. I didn't know what to do or say or where to turn. Obviously the first person I called was my brother. He stepped in, as I knew he would, and left work immediately to run to my side.

The next several months were an emotional hurricane and the beginning of a downward spiral that, over the following one and a half years, led to an almost crippling depression. I lost interest in *everything*. I had no energy or drive, and I pulled away from all my family and friends—and many of them, especially those I thought were my closest friends, pulled away from me. And you know what? I couldn't blame them. To the outside world, I was like, "It's OK, all is good, everything is fine" (insert big smile). But in those moments of solitariness, my world crumbled and I dropped to my knees, a complete basket case.

The only dream I had was of being in a fatal car crash that would end all my suffering instantly. I slept with a bottle of pills in my hand, hoping that I would wake up in the middle of the night with the courage to take them all. But then I would look up at

5

the dresser, and there they were: pictures of my kids. How could I possibly take away their mom? I couldn't. My kids gave me a reason to live. They kept me alive.

By 2009, with the insistence of my immediate family, I sought professional help and was diagnosed with clinical depression. Whoa, who knew?! I thought I'd just been sad. The treatment I started to receive, including talk therapy several times a week, actually helped quite a bit. I was almost back to normal. Until...

Later that same year, when we learned that my brother's brain tumor had returned in a more aggressive state: glioblastoma, stage 3/4. Not good, again. No one survives that diagnosis. But I still believed in the power of prayer, and I believed my brother would fight this again and *win*. The original diagnosis had been for three to five more years of life. He was now in year eight, living an otherwise incredibly healthy and happy life.

The fact was, in my mind, he had to beat this thing, He was my only brother and I needed him in my life, more than ever. There was no way he could leave me now.

For the next one and a half years, I watched my brother fight the battle of his life. Slowly, he lost all movement in the right side of his body, becoming completely paralyzed. The seizures were growing bigger and stronger, each time taking more of his mobility. It was devastating for our family to watch him in this state, especially since there wasn't a damn thing we could do to stop it.

While this was going on, I was also now raising my kids and supporting my family on a single income. During the divorce, I had insisted on staying in my house, the only home my children had ever known. I refused to take that away from them, too. So I practically depleted my entire retirement savings by withdrawing enough money to give my ex-husband half the value of my home. Unfortunately for me, this was just one year before the real estate market tanked, and so the value of my house was the highest it had ever been.

Keeping up with a mortgage on half the income plus raising two kids and a large dog was not easy. I did not get alimony or child support—part of the divorce agreement—so the only way I could keep up with expenses was to supplement my income with credit cards. I did this until I could no longer make the monthly payments, which inevitably led to bankruptcy. In the culture I grew up in, bankruptcy is a *big* no-no. Once again I felt overwhelming guilt, shame and pain about my situation. And I felt that I could never tell my parents.

My entire life, which I had believed at one point to be perfect, was crumbling little by little—first my marriage, then my finances, then my brother's health. You would think that my job could have been a source of refuge during this incredibly difficult time, at best a distraction. But I cared less than ever about work. It felt meaningless, nothing more than a paycheck, and I was growing more unhappy at work by the day. As someone who wears her heart on her sleeve, I'm sure my disposition was evident to most people who knew me, even when I thought it wasn't.

My already clinical depression deepened. On some days I was in so much emotional pain, I would close the door to my office, turn off the lights, crawl under my desk, use my gym bag as a pillow and fall asleep. Thank goodness I exercised religiously, or I'm pretty certain I would not have made it through this time. I had no choice but to accept the medications that the doctors had wanted to give me at the time of initial diagnosis. I gave in and started taking them. And I do believe they saved my life.

My brother passed on February 1, 2011. He was just 37 years old. The miracle was that it had been almost 10 years since his original diagnosis, double the life expectancy that he had been given, and I thanked God for two things: ending his suffering, which had become unbearable to watch, and giving us those extra years together. On February 4, my parents and I should have been celebrating my father's 70th birthday. Instead, we spent most of the day at a funeral home, saying good-bye to my brother.

But David's death didn't just impact my family. It was a tremendous loss for everyone whose lives he had touched. As I mentioned, my brother had been a high school teacher and athletic coach for an inner-city school in Newark, New Jersey. The school has always been home to a large immigrant population, and as such many of David's students came from very humble beginnings and lacked strong role models. As a first-generation American, my brother appreciated the sacrifices and struggles that these young individuals faced. He empathized with and had immense compassion for their stories. A college graduate, accomplished athlete, gifted teacher and award-winning coach—his accolades included numerous state and national championships, and Coach of the Year—David was also for many of his students their only role model: father, brother, mentor, friend. David gave his heart and soul to every one of his "kids," as he called them, and took them under his wings. He endlessly encouraged them, giving them the strength and courage to believe in themselves and their dreams, and to know that absolutely everything is possible if you work hard enough and, in his words, "Never, never, ever give up."

So it was no surprise that two buses packed with faculty and students came to his wake to pay their respects. They brought signs, letters, posters and pictures to hang on the wall next to where David peacefully rested. They came up to my parents and me with tears in their eyes. His students, many now grown adults with children of their own, shared stories about how they would not be where they were without Coach. We knew how special his students had been to him, but we were blown away by how much he had clearly meant to his students, too, and the extent to which he had gone above and beyond, again and again, to help them in their greatest hours of need. Registered nurses, teachers, paralegals, corrections officers and more, all former students of David's, paid their respects and expressed how they owed everything to their beloved Coach.

Listening to their stories, I could not have been more proud and felt more fortunate to have been related to this amazing person and to have had him in my life. The stories filled me with joy and happiness, because they made me realize beyond a shadow of a doubt that my brother would forever live inside the hearts of all his former students.

At the same time, the experience made me take a good, hard look at myself: What had I done in my own life that had been meaningful? What lives had I touched? What difference had I made? What stories would people tell about me, and what positive impressions and memories would I leave behind? I realized with sudden clarity that there was more to life than what I had experienced so far, and that I had not yet even begun to scratch the surface.

Then, on May 4, just three short months—exactly, to the day—after my brother's wake, I arrived at work and was promptly notified that my position was being eliminated due to budget cuts. First my marriage, then my finances, then my brother, now my job. All gone.

After 24 years of blood, sweat and tears for Prudential, that chapter in my life snapped closed, without warning, just like that. I did not attempt to find another position in a different department within the company because I knew in my heart that the timing of this occurrence was no coincidence. I knew then, and I know now, that my brother was sending me the message that it was time to start following my calling, whatever that might be.

I also knew that I needed this push in the right direction because I'm part of a generation of people who are incredibly loyal to their employers. I believe that if my position hadn't been eliminated, I may never have left the company. Fear of the unknown would have held me back. I chose to view this termination as a gift and took the next year to reflect on my life—past, present and future.

During this sabbatical, I focused not on what I wanted to do with the rest of my life, but instead on who I wanted to be and how I wanted to be remembered. As part of my termination package, Prudential graciously provided me with a professional coach to help me figure things out. After several conversations about what I might do next with the skills I had, my coach asked me one of the most difficult questions I've ever been asked: "What makes you happy?" I was stumped. For most of my life, I had been doing everything I thought I should be doing to make everyone else around me happy. That, in turn, was supposed to make me happy, right? But when my coach posed this very simple question to me, I had no idea how to answer it.

I went home and deeply reflected on this. I began to recall the times when I felt most fulfilled and satisfied, outside of my role as a great mom and wife. The experiences that came to mind included empowering young girls to grow into strong, smart, confident young ladies by leading a Girl Scouts of America chapter; leading charities to give to those less fortunate in disadvantaged communities, with countless food drives, holiday gift drives, pet supply drives and more; traveling to Haiti as part of a team to build a school in a remote village through the One Heart for Haiti Mission. These were the things that fueled my heart and soul and gave my life meaning and perspective.

I realized that at work, it was the times when I'd taken part in creating organizational structure and efficiencies that felt most meaningful, because they'd always led to my colleagues feeling happier and more productive and engaged. I suddenly remembered that the title of one of my favorite textbooks as an undergraduate had been *Productivity Through People*. Even at the tender age of 19, with no real life experience, I had the sense that the only way to achieve true success was through people, especially if they were *happy* people. I still believe this wholeheartedly.

One of my favorite quotes has always been something from Zig Ziglar, and it reads, "You can have everything in life you want, as long as you help enough other people get everything they want in life." My revelation that night was that as long as I am able to help other people get everything they want out of life, I will be fulfilled. I had gained clarity about what makes me truly happy—now I just needed to go after it!

I dug into an intense round of internet searching and learned more about the art, science and practice of being a certified professional coach. I enrolled in a program at the Institute for Professional Excellence in Coaching (iPEC), a New Jersey-based institution that is one of the largest coach-training schools in the world and is dedicated to building, supporting and preserving the integrity of the coaching industry. And so, organically, by following my passions and listening to my heart, I became a "coach"—just like my brother.

During this time I also discovered the field of change management, which is the human side of project management. My strong project management skills had served me quite well over the years, but change management sounded much more appealing. Again, I enrolled in courses to deepen my knowledge and training and completed the certification program at Prosci (Professional Science), a Colorado-based independent research company in the field of change management and a world leader in change management research.

You may be wondering, "If you were unemployed, where did you get the money for all this training?" Great question! But where there is a will, there is a way. I swallowed my pride and borrowed money from my parents. I was a single parent with two kids and no income other than my termination package, but I knew in my heart that these courses would point me in the right direction, and my parents were unfailingly supportive.

While I was engaged in this period of intensive self-reflection, soul searching and professional development, I also started networking. I had never done it before. I remember the first time I went to an event for what is now the Association for Talent

Development (ATD, formerly ASTD): I sat in my car for what felt like forever, debating whether or not to go inside. I finally mustered the courage, put a big fat smile on my face, held my head high and marched in.

And guess what? I wasn't the only one there with the jitters. I met several people that night who were in my shoes, and who didn't know anyone at the event. In fact, I met a guy who had been unemployed for more than a year, and who was about to go on an interview at Prudential. It turned out that the person he was interviewing with was someone I knew very well, and who was part of my old department. After talking with him a bit, I got the sense that this guy was exactly what the department needed. So I reached out to my old colleague and submitted a stellar referral for my newly networked contact. And he got the job! Did he get the job because of me? Absolutely not. He got it entirely on his own merit. But did it hurt for him to have a recommendation from me? Certainly not. It felt wonderful knowing that I might have played a part in helping this man land his first job, a great job, in more than a year. I felt energized, empowered and excited to do more and help more people if I possibly could.

It was attending these types of events, and having experiences like the one with the man who got hired by Prudential, that led me to the idea for this book. Although from the moment I lost my job I felt that it was a blessing in many ways, I still in those early days frequently felt alone, scared, deflated and defeated. But whenever I walked into one of those networking events, I was no longer any of those things. As a result of all my networking, I met some extraordinary people and made some truly amazing new friends—wonderful, like-minded, dynamic, kick-ass souls with a passion for spreading love and kindness, and for sharing their gifts and talents with the world. And after talking with many, many other people who had lost their jobs, I realized that there was a wealth of inspiring stories about the experience. I began to understand that if I could just capture some of this, and get it all down in a book, that it might help others going through the pain and confusion of losing a job to not feel so alone. I wanted people to know that others before them had been in their shoes and had gone on to lead happy and productive lives. I wanted to spread *hope*.

While I was staying incredibly active with my professional development and networking, I started to see the months fly by. It had been almost a year since my job had been eliminated, and that meant one thing—the money was running out. But with the job market still in a state of crisis, I decided I would not allow it or my circumstances to take control of my situation. I was determined to take matters into my own hands. I made a list of all my skills, took stock of the enormous amount of experience I had to offer, and took the plunge by starting my own management consulting and coaching practice: Performance Continuum Management Consulting & Coaching. I zeroed in on my core statement—"A consultancy passionate about a singular mission: helping our clients achieve a competitive advantage through their people"—and threw myself into the work of developing a series of customizable learning and leadership programs that covered Social & Emotional Intelligence, Change Leadership, Energy Leadership, Personality Assessments, Executive Life Coaching and more.

Soon I'd done everything necessary to launch my business. And at that exact moment, I got a call from a friend asking me if I would consider taking a position in her company. It was a great company that I had admired for quite some time, and the position was an excellent fit for me. What's more, it was only a 10-minute commute from my home. But it was also two grade levels and 35 percent less money than I had been used to at Prudential. I weighed the pros and cons of taking the role or pursuing my new business, and ultimately decided that, for the sake of my family, the more responsible thing to do was accept the position, because it would ensure a steady income. I put the consultancy on hold, but I never dissolved it.

The job was great, for the first year. Then I started feeling underutilized, undervalued, not challenged. There was so much more I wanted to contribute to this great company and I felt my level of influence was limited because of the role I was in. Still, I worked for some amazing leaders and they kept me content by assigning work on high-profile, high-visibility, large-scale, global transformational projects in addition to my regular duties. I even had the privilege of leading several workstreams and directly supporting one of our regional call centers, a highlight in my career at this company.

This was all wonderful, for as long as it lasted. But all good things must come to an end, and so it did. On July 8, 2015, I learned my position was being eliminated as a result of impending organizational restructuring and a request from the finance department for head count reduction. I knew this was a difficult decision for my boss. I knew they appreciated me and hated to see me leave. Their hope was that with all the relationships I had formed over the years, I would secure a position in another business unit that was not under such strict cost containment. This did not happen; the opportunities just weren't there.

Generally speaking, I'm fairly optimistic and tend to look at situations from a positive perspective. I believe this is still all part of God's great big plan for my life. Being terminated the first time had set the wheels in motion for me to truly follow my passion. Being terminated the second time was what allowed me to plow full steam ahead, with no reservations.

For three years, I had been kicking myself about how long I'd allowed the project for this book that you hold in your hands to drag on. But then on that day, July 8, when I lost my job for the second time, I understood why it had been taking so long: My own story hadn't been ready yet. But now it was. That same night, I received an out-of-the-blue email from a publisher who had heard about my book and was interested in discussing publishing possibilities with me. If that's not affirmation, I don't know what is!

I do believe that our stories all, always, continue to evolve. A new chapter has begun in mine, and it couldn't feel more right. Performance Continuum Management Consulting & Coaching is finally fully up and running, and I am joyfully accepting clients. I am also actively expanding David's Gift, a scholarship program I launched in February 2015, in honor of my brother. It will provide funding to deserving inner-city high school seniors who dream of higher education and making positive changes in their lives.

And last but not least, I have completed this book and put it in your hands. My hope is that if just one story in this book inspires just one person to move in the direction of his or her dreams, then I will have accomplished my goal.

I recently read this excerpt about change by author Radleigh Valentine, and it perfectly captures my hard-earned convictions about loss and change:

"Change nearly always is for the better. It may not feel that way at first, but life is always pushing us towards joy. The path towards joy may be bumpy and it's possible it takes a detour through a very dark and scary forest, but in the end the tangled limbs of trees separate and we come to a meadow of sunny skies. The journey delivers us to a place where we are more empowered, stronger, and closer to our place of happiness in the end. We may leave souls we treasure behind, but there will also be new souls to love at the place we are traveling to. Look at change as a fresh wind blowing at your favorite temperature straight into your face. Challenging you....begging you...daring you to be happy! And then...take the challenge!"

Do I believe that losing my job—twice!—was the best thing that could ever have happened to me? Absolutely. I don't necessarily believe that everything happens for a reason, but I do believe in one of the primary things I learned during my training to become a coach, that "purpose can be found in everything that happens." And I believe that everything that has happened in my life has prepared me for the next thing about to happen. I believe that as long as I continue to make choices that are aligned with my core values, beliefs, hopes, dreams and aspirations, my life will be purposeful and meaningful.

I'm ready to take the challenge. Are you with me?...

"The road to success is not straight.
There is a curb called Failure,
a loop called Confusion,
speed bumps called Friends.
You will have flats called Jobs.
But if you have a spare called Determination,
an engine called Perseverance,
insurance called Faith,
and a driver called Will Power,
you will make it to a place called
SUCCESS."

—Author unknown

CHAPTER 1
DREAM BIG

"My philosophy is that not only are you responsible for your life,
but doing the best at this moment puts you in the best place for
the next moment." —Oprah Winfrey

Here's the thing: I know your head is spinning and that you're dazed and confused over losing your job. But as hard as it is to be out of work, it can also be an unexpected chance at a new beginning. A new direction may emerge out of this experience that will change your life in unanticipated and positive ways.

Going through job loss can be an excellent opportunity to reevaluate your attitudes and outlook. Try to view your job loss from a different lens: What if, instead of focusing on landing your next dream job, you focus on building your dream *life?*

Start with that question my first coach asked me, the one that cracked everything open for me: "What makes you happy?"

Here's another tip—when you walk into your favorite bookstore, which section of the store are you drawn to first (Starbucks not included)? Cooking? Psychology? Self-Help? Business? Something completely different? What does that say about you and your interests?

Search your heart. Listen to the "whispers" coming to you from inside your soul. Keep in mind what Paulo Coelho, author of the best-selling novel *The Alchemist,* said: "You will never be able to escape from your heart. So it's better to listen to what it has to say." It's amazing what you might learn. In this chapter you'll find stories from people who did just this.

And if you're looking for more questions to provoke you on this exploration, refer to the Career Transition Coaching Questions chapter at the end of this book.

Now read on, and be inspired.

JOHN

It was 1988 when I was dismissed from my position as corporate director of human resources for Paulstra CRC, a U.S. subsidiary of Paris-based Hutchinson Automotive. I had been in the role for approximately three years, during which time I was instrumental in leading significant, transformational culture change. This included integrating a change in ownership and management platform following a major acquisition in 1986, developing a comprehensive human resources strategy, reorganizing the organization, negotiating new labor contracts with multiple unions, implementing total quality management, partnering with customers and reinventing many business processes.

I was pivotal in these change efforts—so pivotal that it in fact resulted in the consolidation and elimination of my own job once the work was complete.

The good news is that I had a wonderful mentor during the nine months prior to my dismissal. With executive experience in France, Spain, South Korea and the United States, he was the ideal person to help reinvent the company I had been working for and transforming for the past two years. He was in fact so helpful to me in my development as a transformational leader that I eventually dedicated my book *Agent of Change: Leading A Cultural Revolution* to him.

He was able to give me a bit of a heads up about my possible dismissal—right before he himself was dismissed. This is when I knew something was definitely up. When he first informed me that he was leaving, I was shocked. New management was coming in from the parent company with a strong, dictatorial style. The situation gave me a chance to evaluate my own career options and consider alternatives.

I must also say that this was not a good time for me to be changing jobs or careers—or so it seemed. To begin with, I was in financial debt, and my wife, who was not working outside the home at the time, was pregnant with our second child. We had no second income and very little in savings. Losing my job would be a real curveball.

Fortunately, I had learned a tremendous amount about leading change with faith, courage and spirit, and I was now facing a personal fork in the road that would challenge me to apply many of the same principles to my own situation. It was a true test of character. Would I worry and become anxious? Would fear and stress get the better of me? Or could I remain present, poised and mindful, despite the circumstances? How would a person of true faith respond?

I began by exploring my life calling: What were the major "dots" in my life, and how might I use my intuition to connect these dots to channel my spirit and find my core purpose and passion? How might I combine my innate desires to teach, to create, to design, to lead, to inspire, to grow and to facilitate positive change on the world? What might that look like? Or would it be better for me to play it safe and go back into another management role for a different company?

During the six-week period between my boss being dismissed and me receiving my own notice, I contemplated all these things and seriously considered several options. I polished my résumé and began looking for open positions. I looked into consulting work, both as a member of a reputable firm and as an independent contractor. I read books and listened to countless self-help audios. I even considered going back to school for a master's degree and PhD, which would have been very difficult financially.

These efforts led to several significant "Yeah, buts," as I like to put it. Yeah, but this isn't really a good time to try something new. Yeah, but I have no savings. Yeah, but how will I pay the bills? Yeah, but I have no training or experience in consultancy. Yeah, but I have no master's degree. Yeah, but I have no other income. Yeah, but I am too young to start a company from scratch. Yeah, but who is going to hire an independent consultant who looks like he just got out of high school? Yeah, but I have a child at home and another one on the way.

I contemplated the forces for and against each option. I knew from my training that every option has pluses and minuses—the key is to weigh them carefully. Despite the significant barriers to starting a business from scratch, I decided this option was at least worth a business-planning effort. I drafted a comprehensive business plan aimed at incorporating a new company by the name of Venture Management Consultants, Inc. This effort took several weeks, including research, figuring out the legal options, financial planning and studying how to do it all.

Most of this work was done at night and on weekends, sitting at my desk at home and brainstorming ideas with my wife. It was an amazing feeling. On the one hand, it seemed like a dream. Was this really happening? And on the other hand, it was incredibly exciting. It was like I'd been let out of a cage and allowed to run as fast as I wanted. I suppose for many people this might seem frightening. But I am not this kind of person. I have tremendous faith and somehow always trust that I will land on my feet. I have had many setbacks in my life and with each one I have gained confidence. I find these challenges exciting and inspiring.

I used my business plan to solicit financing and support from banks, family and friends. Like many entrepreneurs, I ran into countless not-interesteds and nos. To me, this simply translated into, game on! The very effort of preparing such a detailed business plan gave me clear insight into what it would take to be successful and quite possibly world famous as an author and consultant. Fortunately, I knew that many people jump before looking, leading to a painful "Oops!" syndrome down the road. In business, like sports, it helps to have a good game plan. I now teach this to my clients and write about it in many of my books.

In June of 1988 I incorporated my business with two other talented managers who wanted to join me when they saw the plan. We all still worked at Paulstra CRC at that point, and both these senior managers saw the potential in my idea. The only catch was that the banks were reluctant to finance the idea, and none of us had the financial wherewithal to do it on our own. I was finally able to secure a private loan for $20,000 from a family member—all of which was eventually returned within three years—and secure lines of credit with two banks, one of which had become a client.

Meanwhile, I was officially dismissed from my job that July, and successfully negotiated a reasonably fair severance package. This gave me just enough time to make it or break it. The pressure was on!

My two business partners chose another route within the first six months. Despite the compelling vision and business plan, it was a significant leap of faith, and in the end they found it easier to play it safe by finding more traditional management roles. Both partners have done very well in their respective careers and I applaud them. I borrowed additional money to reimburse my business partners for their shares of stock in the new corporation. I was now on my own and adjusted the business plan accordingly.

It was tough losing two friends and business partners at the beginning of this long and sometimes lonely journey, but it was also very motivating. I had no excuses for any results that followed, and it was truly exhilarating to have this wide-open field to explore. I felt like a painter standing in front of a blank canvas: "What is it I want to create?" I asked myself. "What colors do I want to use? What message do I want to send?"

The first two years of business were very difficult financially, yet the joy of creating, designing, building and growing a business fueled me with motivation. I was determined to find a way to make this work and my wife was willing to trust me and support me along the way. We even mortgaged our house to invest in a rental property in case the new business failed—at the very least, we would have another place to live, at a considerably lower cost. I felt fearless and inspired. I was living my purpose and my passion. I was giving what I was meant to give. I felt free and alive and truly in-spirit. The trick now was to direct this sacred energy into efforts and activity that would pay off. I had to monetize my mission.

After striking out on countless "sales calls," I began thinking of alternative ways to connect the dots. After all, it was tough selling "transformational change" to companies that didn't really feel the need. It was even tougher selling it without any perceived credibility or maturity. So I borrowed ideas from law firms and seminar companies, shifting the paradigm from "I go to you to sell my services" to "You come to me to learn and be sold." In other words, why not offer a workshop that invites local companies to come learn about leading change, team-building and motivating people? If the offering is perceived as value, perhaps a few companies will want to buy more!

So I created, designed, developed, marketed and delivered my first public workshop in 1989. My mailing list was 500 local companies in west Michigan. Keep in mind that this was long before anyone had access to the internet and social media. I was printing, labeling and mailing brochures. I contracted with a local university for event space and catering and even asked a friend to sit in on my first session to provide constructive feedback. I was willing to take risks, but I wanted to learn from my mistakes.

The first workshop—"Motivating People: The Leadership Challenge"—was mixed. From a marketing perspective, it was great: I built positive relationships with managers from several local companies, and two organizations contracted me to deliver on-site training and follow-up consultations. One of these companies went on to become Michigan Manufacturer of the Year for several years in a row.

From an accounting perspective, the workshop was a loss. It cost more money to produce than it generated. But here is a question I often contemplate: Is it really a loss if in the long run it leads to a return on investment far exceeding the immediate, short-term focus? In other words, if one $2,000 workshop brings in $1,000 of immediate revenue but leads to a "lifetime" revenue in excess of $100,000 with one of the participating companies, who can call this a loss? Sometimes we just have to step back and look at the big picture.

In fact, it was this line of thinking that prompted me to offer workshops in New York, Washington, D.C., Atlanta, Chicago, Orlando, Boston, Philadelphia, Los Angeles and other major cities within two years of launching my company. I simply expanded my mailing lists through organizations like ASTD and SHRM and local chambers of commerce.

It was also this line of thinking that led to my writing and publishing my first book. The title of my second workshop was "Pulling Together: The Power of Teamwork," and I had developed a comprehensive workbook to accompany this course. With a mailing list of now more than 50,000, I was soon getting inquires about "buying the book" rather than attending the workshop. The only problem with this was that I did not have an official book. I had only the workbook that was designed for interactive participation.

I knew I had to write an actual book. In 1993, my first book, *Pulling Together: The Power of Teamwork*, was published. It has since been published by four different publishers in four different versions and is a best seller for one of those publishers, Sourcebooks.

I mentioned earlier that I invited a friend to join my first workshop and provide feedback. The first words from her mouth when I asked her for her comments were, "Do you want the truth?" I now laugh at this response because it was such a tactful way to say, "This might hurt." My friend went on to say that the content was great but the delivery method could certainly be improved—using a traditional lecture format, I'd come off as too directive. She recommended that I apply more creative learning techniques and experiential exercises, and gave me contact information for a source in Minneapolis that specialized in experiential learning, urging me to attend a session. At first I wanted to defend myself, but then I realized that I might be getting in my own way. I enrolled in the training course and have used the lessons I absorbed there ever since. I listened to my friend, I learned and I applied what I learned.

Upon the release of my first book, I was encouraged by one of my brothers to write an allegory. I asked him, "What is an allegory?" He explained that it was like a novel, but was a story often used for education and training. He said that I had an interesting way of telling stories and that he thought this style might serve me and my audience well, then he loaned me his copy of *The Goal*, an allegory that had become quite popular. I eagerly read *The Goal*, and wrote my second book, *Agent of Change: Leading a Cultural Revolution*, as an allegory. The style challenged my creativity and intuition and ultimately led to a book that was endorsed by Dr. Ken Blanchard, one of the best-selling authors and allegorists ever. It was also endorsed by military generals, business leaders, the ambassador to Italy and multibillionaire Richard De Vos. The book really engaged the reader using a very Socratic approach, and it clearly struck a note. I listened to what my brother said, I learned and I applied what I learned.

Among the people who read it was the late Elizabeth Jennings, a retired professor. Betty immediately encouraged me to write a "sequel"—a story aimed at helping people with job dismissal, emotional distress, fear, ego and uncertainty. I listened to her, I learned and I applied. My third book, *Reinvent Yourself: A Lesson in Personal Leadership*, also an allegory, went on to be highly acclaimed by syndicated newspapers, radio interviews and newscasts.

As the years passed, I continued to create, design, develop, market and deliver hundreds of workshops worldwide. I have now trained tens of thousands of leaders in dozens of countries, published 18 books and developed training material that is used by universities and companies everywhere. I have done this through more "subtraction" than addition. While on the surface it seems I have added quite a lot (e.g., new books, materials, clients, etc.), I prefer to think of true empowerment as getting out of our own way. It is more about subtracting the limiting beliefs, doubts, fears and "illusions of the mind" that hold us back. It is about getting past the all too common "Yeah, buts" that we find around every turn. Some of the most significant "Yeah, buts" are self-inflicted. We limit ourselves in so many ways.

Life should be joyful. We are meant to be joyful. The spirit within each of us is joyful. It is fearless and desires to be free. It is limitless and continuously seeking creative expression, growth and manifestation. When we let go of the mental and emotional barriers holding us back, we then let flow with spirit.

Losing a job is often just what we need to learn this and apply it. Like so many other people, I can say without doubt that my own job loss was a blessing in disguise.

ABOUT JOHN J. MURPHY:

John J. Murphy is the Founder and President of Venture Management Consultants (1988). He has authored 18 books and has another on the way. His most recent title is *Zentrepreneur* (2014).

John has trained thousands of people from over 50 countries on topics such as inspiration, high-performance teamwork, personal empowerment, leading culture change and applying Lean Six Sigma methodologies. John is also a highly respected speaker and management coach.

For more information on John's work, go to his website at: www.venturemanagementconsultants.com or follow him on Facebook at www.facebook.com/Author.John.J.Murphy.

KELLY

My journey began on Tuesday, January 20, 2009, at 9 a.m., with an unexpected cathartic shove from the universe. This push came in the form of a meeting with my boss, Terry, who handed me a manila envelope and said, "You have 10 days to review this document with your attorney and sign it."

That simple phrase and action shifted time into slow motion. I could see my boss's mouth moving, but I could not understand the words coming out of it. Dumbfounded, I looked at him and mustered up the courage to blurt out one word: "Why?" Terry's response: "We put your sales numbers through a corporate budget matrix, and you did not make the cut."

His words hit me between the eyes like Thor's hammer, causing my brain to go cloudy and knocking the wind out of me. I responded in a very uncharacteristic way. "That's bullshit and you know it," I said. Terry looked at me with a cold, emotionless stare and said, "You have 10 days to review this document with your attorney and sign it."

I had been laid off. Well, to be more precise, me and my 29,999 colleagues across the world had been part of the company's first round of downsizing.

As I took the envelope from his hand and walked out of his office, thoughts flooded in: Wait! This cannot be happening! I'm a top senior sales trainer and marketer. I've made lots of money for this company. I've helped convert businesses that hated working with us into raving fans, coached my colleagues, become a trusted adviser to hundreds of business owners and executives. I've sacrificed so much of myself to create a successful career, and now it's being ripped away from me?

Getting from Terry's office to my cubicle was like walking through Jell-O. I picked up a few things from my desk and was escorted out of the building. I don't remember the drive from my office to my home. I do remember thinking, "How do I get in touch with Brian?" My husband of six months was on a voluntary deployment with the U.S. Navy to Guantanamo Bay. He had no idea what was going on with me, and I had no way of getting in touch with him.

When I got home, I collapsed in a shame-filled puddle of tears and confusion on our couch, and that's where I stayed for seven days. I didn't shower. I didn't eat. I got up only to take care of our dogs, then I would résumé the fetal position and succumb to the victim thinking and blame spiral: Why me? What did I do? I wasn't just wallowing in my self-pity, I was bathing in it.

On the seventh day, our golden retriever, Murphy, came and put her sweet head in my lap and looked at me with her soft brown eyes as if to say, "It's going to be OK, but you have to get off the couch and shower." And so I did. I got myself up and into the shower, and as I was in there, the floodgates of creative thought began to open (pun intended): Well, those thoughts said, you have a severance package and are able to collect unemployment, so now is the time to do something more life-affirming with your life.

But what? I had no idea.

I knew I needed to start by doing some internal work on myself. My confidence was shaken, and I needed to build myself back up. I went to Steve Chandler's website. Steve is the author of 30 books that have been translated into more than 25 languages. His personal success coaching, public speaking and business consulting have been used by CEOs, top professionals, major universities and more than 30 Fortune 500 companies. I bought his 12-CD success course, "Mindshift." With the purchase of the course, I got a free 90-minute phone session with a coach named Charrise McCrorey. I reached out to Charrise and scheduled the call immediately.

Several days later, on my coaching call with Charrise, I was telling her my sob story about being laid off. I was going on and on about how terribly I had been treated, fully immersed in my victim story. Charrise listened quietly, and about 45 minutes into my rant she asked, "Kelly, are you open to some coaching around this?" I responded, "Of course!" Charrise said, "I think you're a victim and you need to take ownership of your life."

Another statement that knocked the wind out of me! I immediately jumped to the defensive. "Fuck you, Charrise!" I shouted and hung up the phone. Actually, I think I slammed it.

Then something in me shifted, my thinking slowed down and I noticed two questions floating in my mind:

Is she right? Is there any truth to what she said?

Both answers came back, "Yes." When I looked down at my watch I noticed I had 45 minutes left on our phone call. I knew this was my chance to turn my life around and create what I wanted for myself and my family. So, I picked up the phone and called Charrise back. I apologized immediately and asked if we could continue our work. It was the beginning of three and a half years of intense introspection that changed the trajectory of my life.

During that time, Charrise kept pushing me out of my comfort zone like every good coach does, and I found myself working for my certificate to become a business coach. Once I finished that process in 2010, I began to give others the gift that Charrise gave me. The gift of coaching. What I noticed was how happy I was conducting conversations that mattered with my clients. I loved seeing their potential and watching them rise up to meet a challenge.

My husband, Brian, was extremely supportive from the beginning, and our relationship deepened as I became more self-actualized. Two years after Terry fired me, I wrote him a thank-you note saying, "Thank you for giving me the greatest gift one human being can give another: their life's purpose." I am living my dream of holding others and their businesses accountable to the best versions of themselves.

ABOUT KELLY MEERBOTT:

Are you a C-Suite executive who wants to be an inspired leader? Are you looking for more creativity and innovation in your company? Do you lack authentic feedback in your role? Are your team members disengaged? Do you need to clarify your purpose?

Well, Kelly Meerbott is the right person to walk alongside you to co-create solutions and help you remain relevant amid rapid change. In 17 years, Kelly has transformed small businesses, Fortune 500 companies and thousands of lives. She holds her clients accountable for making their dreams happen and helps them take strategic steps towards self-designed success. In every realm, at every level.

Kelly is a guest columnist for the *Philadelphia Business Journal* and a host for Executive Leaders Radio.

For a no obligation conversation with Kelly, call: 757-262-8329 or email her at kelly@youloudandclear.com.

CHAPTER 2
TURN THE PAGE

"There comes a day when you realize turning the page is the best feeling in the world, because you realize there's so much more to the book than the page you were on." —Zayn Malik

The experience of job loss is an opportunity to turn the page. Though having said that, I understand full well that it can be easier said than done. But you can do this. Countless other people have, and you can, too. To begin to muster the courage and confidence to help you "turn the page," consider these tips:

- **List your positives.** Make a list of your positive qualities and your successes. This list is always easier to make when you are feeling good about yourself. If you're not having a particularly sunny moment, enlist the assistance of a close friend or caring relative. Over the course of the next

few days, additional things may pop into your mind—
add them to the list!

- **Replay your positives.** Once you have made this list, replay the positives in your mind frequently. Associate the replay with an activity you do often. For example, you might review the list in your mind every time you go to the refrigerator or put on your shoes.

- **Use the list before performing difficult tasks.** Review your list when you are feeling down, or need extra energy to complete a difficult task. You'll be amazed by how effective it can be to spend a few minutes reviewing your list of positives right before a job interview!

- **Recall successes.** Every day, take some time to reflect more deeply on one of the successes on your list.

KEVIN

(The views expressed here are personal in nature; they are not rendered in a professional capacity, nor do these views reflect those of the U.S. Department of Labor.)

There I sat, two seats to the left of the U.S. Secretary of Labor at an enormous wood conference table in the department's national headquarters in Washington, D.C. Maybe 20 people, like me, without a job—many for the first time in decades—had been invited to a January 2014 roundtable discussion with a federal cabinet official to talk about the trials and obstacles older workers faced as we battled long-term unemployment.

The night before, I'd decided on a plan. Like every plan I had made since 2011, the endgame was the desire to return to work: to find a job. Not a job to satisfy a mortgage on a beach house or finance a BMW, just one that would enable me to avoid eviction and keep my wife, daughter, a Pomeranian named Steinbeck (yes, Steinbeck) and me in our modest New Jersey home.

I chose my seat close to the Secretary carefully. He would probably go clockwise around the room. Don't take the first seat to his left, I thought. In the second seat, I could listen as someone else spoke and I gauged the vibe in the room, deciding if the conditions felt right for what I was about to do. I had written my remarks deliberately, still tweaking words and phrases as I ate lunch briefly before the meeting. Up to the moment the words began to leave my mouth, I was unsure if I was gambling too much. I was about to expose my fears and insecurity before a room of strangers. In addition to the invited guests, chairs lining the walls were filled with federal staff and journalists from *The Washington Post*.

Taking stock of those around me and the situation, I hoped not to appear desperate or, worse still, scary. As the woman to my right spoke, I sipped some tepid coffee and decided I would not leave this room without being sure that the Secretary of Labor remembered my name and my story. I was about to address a man who would share what he heard here with the President of the United States. The next 10 minutes would change my life.

In the three years prior, I submitted applications for hundreds of jobs. I kept a routine, getting up every morning, going to the library or a friend's business where I borrowed a desk. Each week, more than 40 hours—on the phone, sending and replying to emails, completing online job applications, making connections and prepping for countless phone interviews and more than a dozen serious interviews. Several moved to the final round, but all ended in disappointment.

The highs and lows were many. A rise in spirit when a human resources representative asked for a phone interview, elation when a live interview followed. I prepared rigorously: rummaging through the company's website, building a dossier on the employer and its industry, conducting web searches for news and background info about the people I was to meet, looking for any connections I might have at the company or for people I knew who knew people there.

It was grueling work. Finding a job at 50 was the hardest and most stressful job I would ever have. My personal situation was equally difficult. For two years, I tapped my retirement account to supplement what my unemployment did not cover. I kept the mortgage current as long as I could, paid to light and heat the house and tried to maintain some normalcy in our home life. I refused to give up; a father and husband can't.

My motivations were basic. I had, and will always have, an obligation to protect my daughter and wife who, stricken with fibromyalgia—an insidious attack on her immune system—suffers from chronic pain but fights daily to be a caring wife and mother, and who is my biggest fan.

My inspirations were simple: an inner voice reminding me that as hard as it might seem sometimes, someone always has it harder. I lost myself in music, in my car, listening to playlists on my iPod. I fantasized about how those who left me unemployed would suffer similar fates. I changed my cell ringtone to "Sink Hole," a song by the alternative rock band the Drive-By Truckers that tells a dark tale of a man who invites the banker to dinner for a "last walk" around the farm before he forecloses on the family home.

All this kept me going. So did a group of very kind people at the Professional Service Group of Central New Jersey. I began attending Monday-morning meetings and then joined the group to network with other unemployed professionals and refresh my search skills. It was through them I found myself in Washington. The center's then executive director, Ken Hitchner, invited me to join him for the drive to D.C. and a chance to tell my story.

Now here I was, about to bare my soul.

"Good afternoon, Mr. Secretary, my name is Kevin Meyer," I began. "I have worked as a journalist and public relations and communications professional for almost 25 years. In the fall of 2011, I lost my job after 15 years in various management roles. I was able to find employment after four months at 30 percent less than I once made, but then I found myself reorganized out of that position nine months later," I said to establish my bona fides.

"Today, I am unable to pay my mortgage," I continued. "My unemployment benefits have expired. Foreclosure has begun on my home, and, honestly, I don't know where we are going to live.

"I must tell you—even while I do not like to discuss it publicly—that I was diagnosed with an aggressive form of abdominal lymphoma in 2006. It was beaten back by an aggressive course of chemotherapy that left me with permanent neuropathy in my feet and chronic pain," I confided to the room full of strangers. "I am glad to say that my cancer has remained in remission since.

"That said, the last three years of my life have been worse than my cancer. When you have cancer, you get your treatment and hope for the best. There is no treatment for unemployment. I am without a job and losing hope fast. Please tell the President how badly people, like those of us here, are hurting. Thank you for this opportunity."

My remarks finished, the room lay silent. Behind me, I heard sniffles. I had fought through my emotions as I spoke. The Secretary was sympathetic, thanking me for my frankness and offering some thoughts. Stories like mine, he said, motivated him and those in the department to fight on our behalf. After everyone had their chance to speak, we thanked our host and headed home.

Not long after, I accepted a temporary job to process applications from nonprofits for federal funds. The money I earned replaced the long-term unemployment that Congress cut off in December 2013. The job, however monotonous, allowed me to regain some sense of myself, learning new things and showing again how I can exceed expectations. I had missed working with others, talking sports or movies or whatever. I settled into a routine. I met an assortment of people: displaced corporate types slowing the burn on their retirement savings, an unemployed teacher and a few mothers seeking a second income.

I also stayed in contact with Ben, the U.S. Department of Labor official who had arranged the Secretary's roundtable meeting. He was a resource for me when I pursued, but failed to get an interview for, a federal job in New York. Months slid by as whispers of layoffs at my temp job began. In October, the full-timers told us, the number of applications dwindles and people start to disappear. No good-byes allowed; a sudden invite to a late-afternoon meeting brought the unwanted news and an escort out of the building. The pace of work slowed; this temp job would soon end.

One day, on my morning break, I received an email from Ben asking if things had improved. I wrote back that things were bleak, foreclosure was imminent and the threat of eviction, in the weeks near Christmas, was now real. I shared details and frustration in passionate and sometimes angry terms.

A few days later, Ben responded. He was honest and empathetic. He had shared my email with the Secretary, who would ask Ben about me whenever he saw him ever since we'd met. Ben said the department's head of communications would like to speak with me. I arranged what I figured would be a courtesy call the next afternoon. You know the kind—some sympathy, some suggestions and maybe a contact.

The next day I headed to my car during my afternoon break. I listened as the head of the public affairs group said the department's communications needed a dedicated editor. The year prior, the department had issued more than 1,200 news releases, media advisories and statements. Output aside, the communications lacked consistent quality.

As we talked, the opportunity seemed too good to believe. If all worked out, I would be employed by the Labor department in my home office in New Jersey. I was a prime candidate: a combination of skills and experience, my status as a disabled person (thanks to chemo and its aftereffects) and the federal government's desire to expand telework to strengthen its workforce. Interviews were arranged, with multiple phone conversations followed by a trip to D.C. for interviews.

With a week or so to bone up on my knowledge of the department's history and current mandates, I prepped. My train arrived as scheduled and I began one-on-one conversations with senior staff. Running on adrenaline and a deep sense of hope, I hid any sign of desperation as I answered questions, convincing the "jury" that I was the right person for the job.

I soon had a job offer, my first in years. Not another temp or freelance gig, but a meaningful, full-time position with an organization, for a cause in which I have always believed—the value of the American worker.

With my new job secured, I was able to modify my mortgage to keep our home. Long-term unemployment cost me two-thirds of my savings for retirement, something about which I no longer think much. I am grateful we are able to pay our bills and my wife can see the specialists who help her cope better with her condition. I no longer avoid family gatherings and chats with friends because I feel shamed by my inability to get a job. I can now enjoy life's simple things—seeing a movie with my wife and daughter, hearing live music on occasion and watching football on Sunday without worrying about the jobless week ahead.

I recently marked my first anniversary as a federal public affairs specialist. No celebration, no acknowledgment needed, just a smile when I woke that day. Ironically, I was in D.C. for meetings. Just 52 weeks had passed, during which time the department had issued more than 2,200 news releases, statements and advisories. It seemed like a lifetime had passed, a trauma fading in rear view.

These days, I hardly remember the "unemployed" me. Like him, I still wake to an alarm each day. But I have another purpose now. I help tell the stories of a department that ensures people are safe and healthy at work, and that workers are hired and employed without bias toward gender, race, sexuality, age or disability. We show how employers cheat workers out of their wages or don't fund worker retirement plans as promised. We provide skills training to displaced workers and returning veterans to give them new starts. We work globally to combat child labor and abusive and dangerous work practices. Never has the work I do made such a difference.

I am living again, able to exhale and no longer fearful of the future. Unemployment and its wrath was long, hard and sometimes terrible to face. Like the cancer, unemployment tested my character, my will and my desire to survive. While I will always own my inner scars,

I am proud that I passed these tests and brought my family safely through to the other side.

AUTHOR ANONYMOUS
at the writer's request.

NEIL

Once upon a time. like many others, I had aspirations of being highly successful as defined by my career. In my 30s I was doing well and had all the "perks"—the big staff, the big budget, the big title, and I was well regarded within the company. Then the very large company painfully collapsed. It fell from being a $3.2 billion enterprise with 33,000 people to an asterisk in business books and a case study at business schools. Oh, yes, the mighty can fall.

So, 14-plus years were gone, just like that. Interestingly, though, because of what the company once had been, I think that most of us who were there still feel that we were part of something special during those years.

I was able to take my experience and skill and move to another company. It, too, I found, had internal problems that were well concealed from the masses, and in the late 1990s was teetering on the brink of collapse. A huge Japanese company bought us out and we became a new entity—sadly with the same problems. Again, I had, personally, a good ride for the first few years, but the culture was an odd one and everything was centralized at a U.S. corporate level, with all power held by the king. For nearly 17 years I watched multiple organizational and management-style changes take the company lower and lower.

During my last few years at this company, the Japanese owners turned over the reins to the Brits and Aussies, who knew absolutely nothing about the corporate culture we were working in in the U.S., nor did they care. It was painful to watch and be part of, but I, like many, put up with it because we were all too comfortable and complacent to leave. For many irrational reasons, we found it easier to bitch, moan and complain to each other than to find other, more satisfying jobs.

Over time I couldn't take it anymore and began to hold up the mirror to show the failures and disconnects between what people said and what they did (or, more appropriately, what they didn't do). I became a bit too self-righteous and also found that there really wasn't room for my revelations—the status quo is what keeps people in power, and when you have the power, you want to keep it. Disrupting the status quo is a no-no.

So one morning during my regular call with my manager, she told me with her best somber tone that the senior vice president of HR was on the phone and that he needed to speak with me. And that was that.

Did I go through the five stages of grief over losing my job? Not really, because the first stage is denial, and I was certainly not denying what happened to me. Anger? You betcha—at my boss for her lack of support and her willingness to throw anyone under the bus to save herself; at the colleagues with whom I'd worked for many years for not reaching out. In such times, you learn a lot about people.

Within a few days, while still a bit angry, I also suddenly felt free. Within weeks my blood pressure had dropped, and I was sleeping better than I had in years. I began to realize that I was not going to die from this experience, that all things happen for a reason and that all actions have a purpose—I just had to go find mine.

Helpful hands came from friends and even strangers. When I told them I was fired, many of them immediately responded, "Great! Now you can go reinvent yourself," or, "How does it feel to have freedom?" Those comments were a catalyst that moved me ahead.

I also regularly reminded myself of things I had often said to other people in my current position: Cry a river, build a bridge and get over it. Don't wallow in what you can't control or fix. Suck it up and move on.

As a sociologist by education, I was always fascinated by how people tend to stay in bad situations—bad jobs, bad relationships and so on. I used to think, and used to rationalize for myself, that it was based on consistency, comfort, complacency and "the known." But after being laid off I discovered that the real reason is fear. I opened a book from my shelf entitled *Peaks and Valleys,* by Spencer Johnson, M.D., and there it was, a marvelous quote: "The most common reason you stay in a valley too long is fear masquerading as comfort."

AUTHOR ANONYMOUS
at the writer's request.

CHAPTER 3
YOUR REACTION TO LIFE

"Inner peace begins the moment you choose not to allow another person or event to control your emotions." —Pema Chodron

Most of the contributors of stories in this book could have taken the easy way out when they lost their jobs by curling up in a corner or burying their heads in the sand and basically ceasing to exist. But they didn't. Instead, they chose to take responsibility and ownership of their situations. They refused to allow their circumstances to define them—who they were, or what they would become.

Does fear, anxiety and doubt creep in at times? You bet! All of us, after all, are only human. The trick is to not wallow in these emotions or allow them to linger for too long, and to keep pressing forward with a smile on your face.

In other words, fake it until you make it, my friends. It works wonders. And remember this doozy from Charles R. Swindoll: "Life is 10 percent what happens to you and 90 percent how you react to it." Boom!

Here are two more suggestions to help you stay positive during what can be a very challenging time:

- **Surround yourself with positive people.** Socialize with family and friends who are supportive. You want to be around people who will pick you up, not knock you down. You know who your fans are. Find time to be around them.

- **Volunteer.** Give something of yourself to others through volunteer work. Not only will it make you feel useful and worthwhile, you may also actually learn new skills.

CAROLE

One of the great things about social media is reading all the stories about how people have reinvented themselves. I love a good reinvention story and longed for one of my own, even as I continued on the same career path, doing the same type of thing, year after year.

Throughout my career, I've been known as a highly motivated and effective professional, proficient in corporate administration, office management and cross-functional collaboration. I've had experience in for-profit and not-for-profit sectors across diverse functions including human resources, publications, marketing, finance and accounting. Often, my organizational skills and ability to develop and manage multiple projects saved the corporate day.

In the summer of 2011, I knew something was wrong professionally. I was working as a business deposit specialist at a large regional bank. I had been in the position for more than four years and with the bank for nearly 15. My responsibilities included reviewing the bank's small-business accounts to see if we had better products to offer them, and, if a client requested it, reviewing an account to see if we could lower the client's prices while making sure that the bank still made money.

There were many things I liked about that job: the location (so close to home!), my coworkers, my schedule and its flexibility, the fact that my boss was hands-off and was in another state. I liked everything about that job except the actual duties. I was much more at ease when regional management asked me to work on projects such as leading the region's philanthropy projects or developing awards programs for the employees or planning events. Reviewing business accounts was getting boring. The bank had developed a new spreadsheet for measuring the profitability of business accounts. This spreadsheet worked very well for larger corporate clients but was, in my opinion, overkill for small businesses. And honestly, I just didn't understand how we were supposed to use it.

The summer was coming to a close when I realized that I hadn't heard from my boss in months, other than the emails she sent to our team scattered throughout northern Virginia, Washington, D.C., and North Carolina. Typically, we talked once a month and emailed every other week. I started getting nervous when I received an email from her saying we would talk on September 15 when she delivered my six-month review over the phone.

In the weeks before that phone call, I started checking around to see what other positions with the bank might be available. I even checked with the local human resources staff to see what I might do. It was a little unnerving when the employee relations specialist said, "You might just have to let them fire you. You will get a severance, and you'll be eligible for unemployment. Don't feel that you're not entitled to unemployment; the bank has paid lots of money into the system, and it is there for situations like this one."

When my boss and I had our six-month review phone call, it wasn't pretty. I had always gotten great reviews. My most recent review, just a few months earlier, had been good. But during this call I learned that people were contacting other business deposits specialists at the bank because they didn't like the answers I was giving them or because they thought I was wrong. I had referred someone in error to the department that gave out rates for clients because I thought, mistakenly as it turns out, that it would be OK. And I just wasn't getting how to use the new spreadsheets.

My boss was kind and professional in delivering the review and assured me that it was not a performance improvement plan, which was kind of dreaded in the organization. She did say that she'd arranged for another business deposits specialist in another office to help me with the reviews and the spreadsheets and answer any questions I might have.

That part went well, at first. I met with my colleague every other week and found her incredibly helpful and patient. I knew she was reporting my progress to our boss. Then I started getting odd requests from coworkers—for example, an email from a relationship banker, saying, "Please explain in as much detail as possible why you are recommending what you do." That's not something that ordinarily would have been done, and this was a coworker I did not know well.

I knew the colleague working with me had other projects, and that helping me was taking her away from these. So I wasn't surprised when my boss finally told me to just submit everything through her and to cc her on all my business deposits-related emails. Then she kept changing the rules of the game, and I knew I was being set up to fail. So I just let things happen as they were; no need to fight the system.

The Tuesday after Thanksgiving, I got an email from my boss saying that she would be at my branch the following day with the regional employee relations manager, and would I please find a conference room for a meeting. During the meeting—just five days after my 57th birthday—I learned that my job was being eliminated. I had 60 days to find another position within the bank and did not have to accept something more than two pay-grade levels below my current one, or more than 30 miles away from my current location. I would also get two weeks' severance for each year I'd been with the bank, which worked out to 31 weeks of pay. The employee relations guy nattered on and on about health insurance. Had he checked my records, he would have noticed that I did not get my health insurance from the bank. (I had and still have health insurance through my husband's employer, the federal government.) I wish he had checked and looked at my age and thought I might be concerned about early retirement. I should have raised that concern, but even though I knew what the outcome of this meeting was to be, I was still stunned when it happened.

After the meeting, I returned to my desk, locked it up, found my purse and coat, went across the street to my church, found a vacant room and started calling people—my husband, a business deposits colleague in another area, my college-age daughter and son. I went out to lunch with the women in my office, all of them similar ages as me, all of whom did different jobs but had the same age-related, job-retention concerns. After lunch, I went and bought two suits and started arranging job interviews.

Even though some of the job interviews I arranged were for internal positions, I knew damn well that I was not getting another job at the bank. And yet the employee relations manager had said, "Don't spend all your severance money because we'll have another job for you."

A day or so later, I got a call from the outplacement firm that the bank had contracted. The representative asked me what I planned to do, and I told her, "Oh, I need to continue working." She suggested that retirement might be an option, too, which I just brushed off. She told me that I would be hearing soon from a local representative who would meet with me and work with me on my résumé and help me craft a plan for finding a new job. In the meantime, I learned that this firm offered numerous webinars and telephone seminars for job seekers. Those turned out to be the most helpful thing about the outplacement firm.

Over the next six weeks, I finished up all my projects and transitioned the reports I'd been preparing for years. I started working just in the mornings as I continued going to interviews. None of the positions I interviewed for were things I would have enjoyed for very long, but I enjoyed meeting the interviewers very much.

Finally, on January 30, 2012, my last day, I sent an email to all the coworkers I knew well saying that I was leaving and not sure what was next, but that I'd keep them posted. I had an exit interview with the regional president. I went out to lunch with the same coworkers from the day in November when I lost my job, turned in my key to the office manager and went home.

On February 1, I had my first meeting with the outplacement counselor. It was a gray, rainy day, and I had to drive 20 miles in rush-hour traffic for our meeting. When I got there, I waited for at least 15 minutes before the outplacement counselor finally appeared. My first impression was that she just looked awful, like she was recovering from the flu or had just received some devastating news. My first thought was, if she's not feeling well for whatever reason, she should have called to reschedule. I certainly would have understood.

Our meeting did go well. She explained that I would need to revise my résumé according to their firm's specifications. What that meant was that I had to put everything I ever did on my résumé, back to the beginning of my career. It was 2012—what did it matter what I had done in 1976?! She also explained about the firm's webinars and phone seminars and suggested which ones I should schedule as soon as possible. This was expected to be a three-month process, at least, and we would meet every two to three weeks.

So I went home, worked on my résumé, participated in quite a few phone seminars and webinars, applied for unemployment, stated searching online for jobs and enjoyed the time to myself while my husband was at work. Our kids were away at college, and it was just me and the dog for 10 to 11 hours every day.

My meetings with the outplacement counselor continued going well, but I think she was a bit put out that I had had human resources experience and knew what I was doing. Also, I was not in the market for a managerial or executive position, which was something that seemed to annoy her too. Eventually, I canceled a meeting due to illness, and she never got back to me to reschedule.

Sometime toward the end of March, I got a phone call from a representative of the bank's corporate human resources department: "Would you like to retire?" Hell yes! It turned out that I would meet the conditions of age and years of service in April, and since I was on severance I was still technically an employee. My retirement was effective May 1, and I continued to receive the severance. My retirement paycheck is very small, but at least I am getting one.

My husband's 62nd birthday was at the end of that April. Just a few weeks before his birthday, he told me that he wanted to retire that coming summer. I panicked. Where in the world were we going to get the money? How would we live? I *had* to get another job, and soon!

What I should mention here is that I really had nothing to worry about. Our house was paid off, our cars were paid off, and we used our credit cards for convenience and paid them off every month. We had savings, we had investments earmarked for retirement. And our kids' tuition for their final year of college—both graduated in December 2012—was being paid by a combination of loans, scholarships, and the proceeds from two inheritances we'd received. We had excellent health insurance, which we have been able to keep. But I just couldn't see that at the time.

Meanwhile, I started volunteering in the community, writing press releases for a local not-for-profit organization and serving lunch after weekday services at my church. I joined a local writers' group and became treasurer. I was finding things to do.

That July, I got a call from a former colleague, suggesting that I submit my résumé to a client who had asked if she knew any administrative employees. I emailed my résumé immediately and heard from a representative of the company within the hour. She asked a few questions and told me I'd hear from the company's president.

It turns out that the company is a woman-owned firm that places employees in government contracts. I was offered a position as a part-time business-development specialist, with my initial focus on creating the company's social media presence. I started that job on July 31, 2012, the day after my husband's retirement from the federal government.

And no, the story does not end there.

While I enjoyed working with this company, it was clear that the president did not know what to do with me. Eventually we changed my position to a PR/communications specialist position, and I had to work fewer hours, but that was actually OK.

For a while, anyway. I could work from home, but was getting bored working just five or fewer hours per week. The community choir I sang in announced that they were looking for a part-time director of operations, so I applied and got the job. The first year was volunteer, but the second year I was paid a pretty nice salary for working about 10 hours per week.

At the same time, the yoga studio I went to announced that they needed a work-study desk person for the Friday-morning class. I got that position, which led to my enrolling in the yearlong yoga teacher training course being offered at the studio. To say that I worked hard in teacher training is an understatement. I felt like I was earning a master's degree! During teacher training I was offered and took the position of part-time office manager of the studio.

So there I was, working three part-time jobs and learning to become a yoga teacher! My life was finally changing.

My teacher training colleagues were not just all bankers from the Washington, D.C., area, they were from all walks of life—a writer, a rocket scientist (yes, at NASA), a physical therapist, a stay-at-home mom, a government employee, a human resources recruiter and a CPA, to name a few. And they were from all parts of the country. We learned a lot from our instructors, and we learned a lot from each other.

In fact, we created such a close community that when the yoga studio owner announced that she was retiring and closing the studio, one of the other trainees opened another studio nearby. Most of us are now teachers at this studio. I feel like I finally know the bonds of friendship that I never felt with my sorority sisters in college or in the alumnae chapter.

About the same time the initial yoga studio closed, I left the position with the choir. Yes, it meant that I made less money, but that felt OK now.

Today, I continue my very part-time work with the government contractor, teach two to four yoga classes a week, play the piano and organ for church services and have edited two books for a local author. I'm not making a lot of money, but it's not about the money anymore. I have time to spend with my husband, I have time to go to the gym. One of my students said it best when she said, "Your life is probably more fulfilling now that it's ever been." She is right!

Throughout this process, I have learned a lot about myself. If I'd been able to find another job within the bank, I would have continued working. In fact, that was my plan—work until at least age 64. Once my kids were done with college, I was going to save everything I possibly could so I could travel in retirement. Since I will never have those extra years of savings, my travel dreams have been subdued, but I was able to go to Rome with my sister for a few days this fall thanks to her employer. Now I want to travel even more! And I intend to do so; I just need to figure out the financial piece of it.

The past four years have been filled with a lot of experiences that I would never have had in the corporate world. Am I ready, at age 61, to say, "Thanks for eliminating my job?" Well, probably not. But you know what? I'm grateful for all the opportunities provided by the loss of my job. I can't wait to see what comes next.

ABOUT CAROLE KEILY:

Carole spent 30 years in the banking industry in Washington, D.C., and Northern Virginia. After her banking job was eliminated at the end of 2011, she found new joy in writing and editing and in her music. Carole is now a yoga instructor and editor and is co-developing *Smoke Break Stories*, a series of short stories about big-box store employees on their work breaks.

Contact Carole at: smokebreakstories@gmail.com.

SAMANTHA

I lost my job, and it was the worst day of my life. Well, at least I thought it was the worst day of my life. You see, when you go to college and get that degree (with a side of student loans), you think you can accomplish anything in this world. That's what we're taught, right?

I attended school for broadcast journalism. I always knew I wanted to be in television/radio production and writing. This career position is easily the hardest goal to achieve in Chicago because these types of jobs are very limited. So when I landed a job writing about entertainment, I was ecstatic. It was my dream job. I mean, hello, who doesn't love guilty-pleasure Hollywood news?

The day I landed this job was one of the best days of my life, and I felt like I wanted to work at that organization forever. Everyone would ask me, "How's life?" and I would reply, "I love it. I love my job!" Now that I look back, I am amazed that my life revolved so much around my job at that time, when there is so much more to being alive than working 9 to 5.

After five months of passion, praise and hard work at the company, I was let go due to cutbacks and new management. My heart shattered to pieces. I ran home crying. I was lost, because I thought I'd had it all and that it had suddenly been yanked out from under me. But what I began to realize was that I actually had it all *before*

I took that job—a supportive family, amazing friends, a loving boyfriend, a beautiful place in the city and pure love for my creative work.

What killed me the most after losing this job was that I was no longer financially stable. I had no plan, and I didn't know what to do. I thought that job was exactly what I wanted in life, and I no longer had it. It had slipped out of my hands. That pain lasted months. My heart ached, my motivation was gone and I felt dead inside.

One morning I woke up and was suddenly over the fact that I was sulking in my sadness. I needed to get back into my writing groove. I needed to reconnect with that passion. I packed my bags and went off on a two-week trip. I'm young. I had saved a good amount of money, and I had nothing else to do (except apply for jobs). I felt the need to see the world.

As a writer, I get a lot of my creativity from exploring. Travel helps me shape what I want to do in life—namely, continue to write. I thrive off adventures, and you're limited to how many of these you can have when you are locked away in a cubicle.

It's funny how time really does heal all wounds. After getting let go, I felt numb. I was so scared that I didn't know what tomorrow had in store that I constantly felt nauseated. I was terrified by the prospect of never being happy in my career again.

But as time went on, I figured things out, including that while I was busy crying over the loss of my "dream job," I was missing out on what life was really about: identifying and pursuing my actual dreams. I'd always fantasized about having my own entertainment website. Losing that job gave me the strength to launch my own successful news website, Celebrity Slice. Now I make money doing exactly what I love.

I guess you can say that I accomplished a lot during my time off from work. I learned that applying to jobs feels more natural than ever because I am more aware of what the corporate world is looking for. I learned that spending time with my family is where I find most of my happiness. And after getting back in my groove, I found the strength to be more persistent than ever. I hate to say it, but life is not easy. It's a test. At 23 years old, I realized the most important thing about life: If it kicks you down and you find a way back up, you can do anything you set your mind to.

AUTHOR ANONYMOUS
at the writer's request.

CHAPTER 4
BE THANKFUL

"Gratitude can transform common days into thanksgivings, turn routine jobs into joy and change ordinary opportunities into blessings." —William Arthur Ward

I believe the secret to having it all is knowing that you already do. Every day, give thanks for all the wonderful things in your life, the things that are going well and even the things that are not going so well. Why also the ones that are not going so well? Because these are the things that are challenging you and helping to define whom you will become. They are shaping your character, making you stronger, and preparing you for something even bigger and better.

Consider keeping a gratitude journal. Scientific evidence supports the idea that journaling provides unexpected benefits, such as removing mental blocks and allowing you to use all your brainpower to better understand yourself, others and the world around you. It can improve your resilience and your ability to manage emotionally challenging situations.

The researchers Stephanie Spera, Eric Buhrfeind and James Pennebaker conducted a study whose findings were published in *The Academy of Management Journal* in the summer of 1994. They worked with three groups of people who had been laid off from their jobs. An experimental group was told to write about "their deepest thoughts and feelings surrounding the layoff and how their lives, both personal and professional, had been affected." A writing control group was instructed only to write about their recent plans and activities. Both these groups wrote for 20 minutes every day for five days. A nonwriting control group received no instructions.

Eight months after this five-day period, 27 percent of the nonwriting control group had found new jobs—versus 48 percent of the control group. What's more, a whopping 68 percent of the experimental group who had written about their deepest feelings had found employment.

If you're not sure where to start, keep it simple. Try: "Today I am feeling thankful for…" and continue writing until you run out of things to say. Set time aside every day for this, to pay close attention to what you are experiencing and give voice to what you are feeling.

VALERIE

Being steadfastly employed for nearly 12 years and then being given four months' notice before losing my financial career was initially a very bitter pill to swallow. No amount of sugar coating made it any sweeter. But upon reflection I have realized that we are all evolving spirits, and this was one step along my path.

At the time of my dismissal I was in a supervisory role, managing a team of up to 15 people and producing a variety of reports for internal and external stakeholders. It wasn't exciting work but my salary was good, enabling me to pay my bills with enough left over for indulgences such as shopping and traveling.

I did not realize that the company was in any kind of financial trouble, especially as a new division had just been established in the U.S. But when a new management team was brought in to facilitate the whole termination operation, things became too obvious to ignore. When I found out this team's sole role, I felt wounded, as though they were disregarding and disrespecting my long-term loyalty. Plans for my future outside of work were not mapped out. I was completely accustomed to only thinking as a subordinate, as an employee.

And then, one day in 2003, my employers officially announced their decision to lay off hundreds of employees, me among them.

With the support of a group of trusted colleagues, I began to realize that losing my job was a catalyst. My thoughts and fears about my future became less angry and selfish, and much more positive and bright. As the countdown to my leaving day continued, I walked into the office every day, sat at my desk, logged onto my computer, pulled up the online calendar and made a red cross through the date. I began to feel as if there were no longer any constraints to fulfilling my dreams of starting my own business.

When our release date finally arrived, my colleagues and I had a marathon lunch session in several local pubs. I look back on that day with a big smile; when I left the building, I felt total freedom. I walked away a changed and happy woman with no regrets.

The first few months of unemployment, my "employee thinking" began to shrink. I made rest and relaxation my paramount objectives, as well as attending many newly discovered personal-development seminars. I started to find a whole new way of connecting and communicating with like-minded people. These new associates were also ex-employees or had recently formed small businesses. I felt as if I had discovered a whole new world. All these new connections and experiences came together synchronistically to help move me forward.

In January 2004, I founded my business, Focusivity, which helps people manage their stress levels with positive-energy techniques and strategies. In conjunction with counseling, coaching and mentoring, this practice provides people with practical well-being and stress-relief solutions.

Over the intervening years, my achievements have become less academically focused and more centered on continual personal-development and overall evolvement. I have become more spiritual and more fully aligned on both professional and personal levels. This is reflected in my mutually beneficial communications and all-round connectivity with others.

With the explosion of the internet and the continual development of social media, I knew that these would be powerful tools for reaching thousands of people on local, national and international levels. As a result, I was inspired to create Internet Traffic List Building, the online marketing arm of Focusivity and a platform that helps business owners become more visible and profitable within their target markets.

I had always wanted to care for and nurture others with positive energy, and the time finally came to share what I had to offer. It was like cooking up a sustaining, swirling pot of recipes and goodies known as business-growth solutions. In my world, the word "communication" is a combination of networking, collaborations, connections, meetings, business opportunities, propositions, joint ventures and strategic alliances. All these things are mixed together in a big silver pot to make a lovely, nourishing soup of business-development resources and tools.

Over the years, as my business grew, there were still three things I wanted to achieve: writing a book, broadening my portfolio of services—and getting up close and personal to a Bentley!

The Bentley got ticked off my list when I went to a showroom with my sister and the staff there gave us permission to snap some photos of me in a $200,000-plus Bentley Continental GT. I still treasure those photos.

In June 2012, I wrote the first draft of my book in two hours. I felt divinely guided. Every word seamlessly flowed. I felt powerful, inspired and fearless.

I achieved the third goal with my self-published guide *Be The Confident You! The Inner Battlefield To Great Thinking and Straight Talking.* Its purpose is to help people, especially women, be more confident when attending networking events or gatherings on their own, and to leverage this increased confidence to help them achieve their personal or professional objectives. I drew heavily from my own experiences to craft and produce it.

I've also branched into the real estate sector, an area that has intrigued me ever since I was a child. It has been a natural fit for me, as my role is to bring sellers and their properties to buyers' attention. In other words, I am a matchmaker, a connector. I've also built a network of like-minded businesses that can learn from one another and help each other's business grow. The many years I'd already spent developing my networking and communication skills helped tremendously as I transitioned into this new endeavor.

Last year I took all my experience and my desire to build supportive communities to the next level, and founded AlueStar UK Ventures Limited, a company devoted to business-to-business (B2B) strategic connections and communications, and to maximizing income generation for all involved. I have never felt more entrepreneurial and confident. I am working from my core strengths, combining people, technology and finance to form organic communities, and leveraging that to help others to realize their professional goals.

One of the key things that I stress is that everyone can have an off day, and it's crucial to remember this while building a business or developing a network. A mantra I created and developed addresses the activity of connecting with new people and forming mid- to long-standing relationships. It goes: Give someone a second chance to make a better first impression!

What are the five things that helped me most as I was transitioning from my old company and becoming empowered enough to pursue my own dreams and goals?

Here they are:

- Believe in yourself, even when the doubts creep in
- Only have compatible associates and partnerships
- Seek expert advice whether you have a budget or are bootstrapped
- Always be open to educating yourself and using that to help/support others
- Treat others as you expect and demand to be treated

In retrospect, losing my job was the best thing that ever happened to me. It allowed me to fully be myself and build a business around my strengths. I now feel continually empowered, and this enables me to work with people in a mutually supportive, connected way.

ABOUT VALERIE LOTHIAN:

Valerie Lothian is a strategic communicator, problem-solving accredited mentor and author who enjoys connecting with others and providing tailored solutions to business-development challenges.

Valerie's articles are published in various (offline and online) media outlets, and she is currently building her portfolio of value-add services in the Internet of Things, for example IoT sector for community health care.

Valerie can be contacted directly via her LinkedIn profile www.linkedin.com/in/valerielothianinternettraffic.

CHAPTER 5
CHOOSE FAITH

"Dear Past, thank you for your lessons. Dear Future, I'm
ready. Dear God, thank you for another chance."
—www.quotediary.me

In the preface, I wrote a little about hope as it relates to faith in
my opinion. But what is faith, really? Well, I think the best way
to describe it is with an example:

- Hope sounds like this: I hope I can get through this
  difficult time; I hope I get that interview; I hope I land
  the job of my dreams.

- Faith sounds like this: I will get through this difficult
  time; I will get that interview; I will get land the job of
  my dreams.

As I recounted in my own personal story in the introduction, I went through a very dark time in my life, instigated in part by job loss. The person I had always been disappeared, spiritually, emotionally, even mentally to some extent. During that time, when I was blinded by my own darkness, my parents and brother never lost faith in me, even when I had absolutely no faith in myself. They would say to me, "We have faith that you will pull through this and that we will get our daughter and sister back." They had no doubt that this would be the case. Prayer was a big part of their lives at that time.

So you see, with faith, you don't need proof or evidence of any kind, you just believe something—in your heart, in your soul, in your mind. You release all negativity, doubts and fears to your higher power, whatever that may be for you. You know you were not put on this earth for your story to end this way. No, sir! This may be the end of a chapter in your life, but it is also the beginning of your best seller.

Believe that everything happening in your life today is serving a greater purpose, and that it is all part of your higher power's big plan. Believe it, trust it, know it! That's faith!

PAUL

It was 2010, and I was approaching my 25th year with the same company. My career had taken me through a number of different assignments in several locations and, for the most part, all of them had been successes. I worked long and hard to ensure that I was earning my salary and contributing my best to helping achieve the goals established by my employer. I can't remember ever working a 40-hour week, and frequently brought work home to do in the evenings or over the weekend. And I was always available by email or phone. I had achieved a level of competence that prompted people from our corporate office and counterparts from other field offices to call upon me for advice, information and other forms of assistance. At almost 60 years of age, I had begun to think about retirement, but always in the not-too-distant future.

One day, I was called into a meeting. Little did I know that from that moment forward my life would never be the same. At the meeting I was informed that I was being retired, a few years earlier than I had intended. Suffice it to say that my career was over and, at my age, the chances of getting another full-time position were very slim.

I was also divorced and, because of my very demanding job, had neglected my health. I wasn't sleeping well, I got very little exercise and had been losing my lifelong battle with weight problems for some time. Like most 60 year olds, my body was beginning to rebel against years of neglect. I had back problems, I was feeling the effects of arthritis and, compounded by my weight, I was unable to stand for even a few minutes without being in pain.

So there I was: old, infirm and unemployed with very little hope of a way out of the depths to which I had sunk. This was certainly not the life I had anticipated as a young man.

When I was a young boy, I had a profound religious experience shortly after my father's death (he died at age 59, my age when I had the career-ending meeting). I was about 11 years old at the time and, being so young, I had no idea what to do with this experience. As I look back through the eyes of a now-mature man, I see that I spent much of my life trying to regain that experience. In my 20s, I tried "sex, drugs and rock 'n' roll," to borrow a popular phrase of my youth. In my 30s, I tried family and career as a means to reclaim that experience. This was the start of my workaholic habits, and I never looked back. In my 40s, I added self-help books and tapes, then new-age courses in my 50s. Unfortunately, none of these proved to be the things I needed to fill the void in my life. Then, in my late 50s, I found my way back to active practice of my religion.

At this point, you may find yourself asking what this has to do with my forced early retirement. Well, one answer is, nothing, but it does have everything to do with the way I dealt with the loss of my career. Although I was devastated by the loss, I remember right from the start feeling thankful that I realized that my life was about much more than my work. As dedicated as I was to my job, I did not draw my sense of self-worth from my professional position. I knew there was much more to life than that.

I was also very grateful that I was eligible for retirement and that I had been given a severance package. This meant that at least I would not have to panic about finances. I had some time to discern what this next chapter in my life would be about. Given my health, I knew I would not be able to go on job interviews. Additionally, my doctors told me that stress contributed to my ailments. I decided to apply for, and wound up qualifying for, state disability benefits. They were only available for six months, but that would prove to be enough. I went for physical therapy, and I joined Weight Watchers while on disability.

I also used this time to consider what I would do next. I surveyed the job market and talked to everyone whose opinion I valued (and many whose opinion I should not have valued). And I prayed…a lot. I asked God for wisdom to discern the right path for me. I knew I could not go back into the type of job I had had, although that would have been the logical thing to do. In fact, given the network I had developed over the years, I received offers. But I needed to take a different approach.

I also knew this would make it much more difficult to find a new position. It's hard enough to change careers when you are young. To do so at age 60 is madness! Most people advised me to get my résumé out there and to use the professional networks I had developed to find another j-o-b, but a few wise souls advised me to follow my heart and do something that would have meaning for me.

As I mentioned, I had gone back to active participation in my religion several years earlier. I had become an active member of my parish and an avid reader. My faith deepened, and I noticed that people tended to seek me out to talk about matters of faith. During this time, a chance conversation with a friend, also a person of faith, brought me to the subject of spiritual direction. I had always assumed that one had to be an ordained religious leader to become a spiritual director, but my friend assured me that this was untrue. I did some research (thank God for the internet!) and prayed for wisdom and guidance. A few months later, I enrolled in a spiritual direction formation program at a local spiritual center run by the Sisters of Christian Charity. At this writing, I have completed one year of the three-year program to earn a certificate in spiritual direction.

I have continued to read and deepen my faith. I read the Bible, spiritual books, biographies and history books. I have been participating in and leading small faith-sharing groups in my church, and I am beginning to reach out beyond the boundaries of my parish community to the larger Christian community in my state.

Concerning my physical challenges, physical therapy was, for me, moderately successful. I experienced some improvement in my range of motion and flexibility. More importantly, I have been a Weight Watchers member for more than a year and have thus far lost 111 pounds (I still have more to lose, but I am confident that I will reach my goal weight).

I have to be careful about my finances, but I am learning that I don't really need the six-figure income that I had thought would be the answer to all my problems. I am learning to live a better quality of life on a smaller income and am confident that I will find a way to supplement my retirement income sufficiently to live comfortably but not lavishly. My life is much simpler these days, but I wake up thankful for each sunrise, for each rainstorm and for each new day that has been given to me.

And I am constantly amazed at how life always seems to work out. I always feel that, if you listen carefully, God will nudge you in the right direction. As unemployment and my severance package had run out and I was dipping into my retirement savings, I began to worry. I shared my concerns with God one day during prayer, as I often do. I wasn't actually looking for a specific answer to my problem, just sharing what was on my mind. My plan was to finish the next two years of school and, with my ability to do spiritual direction, look for some part-time work connected with a church or something.

About a week or so later, I happened to be talking to a priest friend of mine who had just assumed responsibility for the retreat center at a Benedictine abbey near my home. I had been working with a group of men from my parish for some time to develop a men's retreat and he had some questions for me. When I asked him about the change in responsibilities at the center, he said he had taken over temporarily, until he could find someone else to run the place. He added, "I'm looking for a lay person."

Well, one thing led to another, and I am now the director of the retreat center. I'm not earning what I was in my "corporate job," but I am earning enough that I will be able to live my life without tapping any more into my retirement savings and without beginning to receive Social Security. More importantly, the abbey is supportive of my educational goals and allowing me time off to attend classes.

And, best of all, when I go to work, I don't feel as though I'm actually going to work at all. I'm doing work that I love in a much less stressful environment. I'm using many of the skills I developed in the corporate world. I'm grateful for all the training I received throughout my career, and I'm especially grateful that I was forced to retire early. Perhaps I should go back and thank the person who made the decision to force me into retirement? Nah!!!

For me, the truly amazing thing is that all this happened with very little effort. I entered into this phase of my life with no idea where it would lead but with faith that it would lead somewhere and that it would be good! I never cease to be amazed at the way God works in our lives. He did not cause my physical problems, and He certainly did not cause me to be forced into early retirement. But both of these problems have, in retrospect, been blessings for me. He has figured out a way to transform these issues into positive forces in my life. He has figured out a way to take years of poor choices on my part and years of developing skills in my career to show me a way to use them to make a difference in the world.

I think my experience can be instructive for anyone trying to bounce back from the loss of a career late in life. We can look at it as a catastrophe (I certainly had my "catastrophe" moments), or we can look at it as an opportunity for resurrection. I'm not entirely certain where all this is leading me, but I know I can never go back to my old way of being. I must confess that I occasionally fell into a shoulda, woulda, coulda mentality, but I tried very hard to make those moments as brief as possible.

If I have any advice for someone in similar circumstances, I would suggest you focus on the positives. If I've learned anything from this experience it is that I am not unique. People in their 50s and 60s are forced into unfortunate circumstances every day. You can't take that as a negative assessment of your worth as a human being. We have much to offer prospective employers. We have much to teach others. We've spent a lifetime learning, and we bring great wisdom to new positions. I realize that my new employer is as lucky to have me as I am to find a new opportunity…maybe even luckier.

At this point in my life, I feel as though I have no time for lamenting over past decisions. There is nothing I can do about the past. I also have precious little time for worrying about the future (since most of what I would worry about will never happen). I try, instead, to focus on the present moment. There is very much that is beyond our control, but attempting to live each moment as it is happening gives me more control than any other strategy.

The end of my story has yet to be written, but I have come to realize that the end of the story is not the important thing. The *story* is everything! The more I worry about the end, the less I actually live the story. And the story is everything!

ABOUT PAUL COCCO:

Paul Cocco lives happily in Morristown, New Jersey. He is the Director of the Retreat Center at St. Mary's Abbey, also in Morristown. In that capacity, he arranges both individual and group retreats for people of all faiths. He is also a retreat presenter, small group facilitator and is available for personal and group spiritual direction.

He can be contacted at 973-538-3231 x2100 or at
retreatcenter@delbarton.org.

CHAPTER 6
LEARN SOMETHING NEW
EVERY DAY

"If you are not willing to learn, no one can help you. If you are determined to learn, no one can stop you." —rawforbeauty.com

With every setback I've experienced, I've immersed myself in personal-development and educational books, workshops and retreats—Tony Robbins, Dr. Wayne Dyer, Oprah Winfrey, Jack Canfield, Jim Rohn, John Assaraf, Brené Brown, Cheryl Richardson, Elizabeth Gilbert, Marrianne Williamson, Shawn Achor, John C. Maxwell, Simon Sinek, Joel Osteen, the list goes on and on. I've come to realize that learning and growth are surefire ways to push myself through a difficult situation and emerge into the next place I'm supposed to be.

There are opportunities to learn all around us. Professional industry organizations offer workshops, seminars, webinars and, very often, at low to no cost (ask for "in transition" rates). The Department of Labor and a number of organizations dedicated to helping those unemployed provide all kinds of opportunities for continuing education. Find out what is offered in your state, and take full advantage of it.

And oh, by the way, if you have the good fortune of landing a job in a company that offers tuition assistance, view it as a bonus because that's what it is!

Check the Resources section at the end of this book for more recommendations about how to continue learning and growing.

KIM

All my adult life, I had never had my work ethic brought into question. I had always worked hard and by the book. I set a very high standard for myself and never gave any company I worked for reason to fire me. When I left a place of employment, it was always on good terms.

I had been working for the same retail establishment for 17 years. I was in a management position and felt at times that I really needed to move on, but I always hesitated. I made a great income, and I had a lot of seniority and great benefits. I'd had lots of experience, knew my job and was doing it well.

At one point, my employer began cutting back staff, and things got very, very stressful. I was working 10 to 12 hours a day trying to pick up the slack. My health was deteriorating, I was spending less time with my family and I was in a cycle of work, eat, sleep, then get up and do it all over again.

Even though I knew this pattern wasn't good for me, I only had 10 more years until retirement, and I planned on sucking it up and sticking with it until then. But my annual review in 2014 unceremoniously burst this bubble. I was put on a 60-day warning and busted my butt trying to save my job. But I began to realize that there were forces working behind the scenes other than my boss to try to get me to leave. Sometimes we're so stubborn that at first we can't see what's directly in front of us.

I understood that God was telling me that since I wouldn't quit on my own, he was aligning things to force my hand. By the time I was halfway through my warning period I had started making plans for how I would manage without a job, because there was no question—they were determined to fire me.

All my planning proved fruitful. On the day I was let go, I immediately went into the ladies' room and did a happy dance. What a relief to be done with all the worrying and stress, and to be happy about it!

After two weeks of "vacation," I started to think about what I wanted to do with the rest of my life. I knew without a doubt that I did not in any way, shape or form want to go back into retail. Believe me, it's a hard life! So what else could I do? I started to look into what might be out there. One day the words "life coach" popped up. I researched that and realized it was something that I could do. I dug up information about schools and determined the best choice for me, then attended a three-day training session. Afterward, I immediately signed up for the full course.

Ten months later and here I am, a certified professional coach and Energy Leadership Index Master Practitioner, at the age of 57. Me! Who knew?! I am so darn proud of myself. For too long I had stayed in a miserable job that I hated because I didn't think I was good enough to do anything better. I almost lost my marriage because I let my job take first place instead of my husband. I missed a huge portion of my son's formative years because I was always working. I missed many special family occasions over the years, all in the name of work. I struggled through severe depression, health issues and myriad other difficult moments—for what? To get fired? To lose faith? To think I'm not good enough?

We always have a choice. Our choices are guided by our thoughts. Our thoughts control our universe. How do you want your universe to spin? Don't let it spin out of control. Have faith, curiosity and hope. Gain confidence and strength. Think about what it is you really want and go for it. The only person stopping you is you.

ABOUT KIM CORCORAN:

Kim is a Life and Energy Leadership Coach helping women make intentional choices to move forward in their lives. She was born and raised in a small town in upstate New York and currently lives in New England with her husband and son.

You can contact Kim at kim@kimcorcoran.com if you would like to find the you that you have kept hidden at your core since becoming a wife, mother and worker bee.

CHAPTER 7
NETWORK, NETWORK, NETWORK

"If you want to go fast, go alone. If you want to go far, go with others." —African proverb

Networking is critical to finding a new job. And it is so much easier than you think! It may sound intimidating or difficult, especially when it comes to finding a job or asking for help, but it doesn't have to be.

Networking can be rewarding and fun, even if you're shy or you feel like you don't know many people. You will meet people just like yourself, and people who at one point were exactly where you are now. You will learn so much from the contacts you make networking; you will be empowered by these people, and in turn empower them. You may even help some people get back on their feet, and I can tell you from firsthand experience that this feels great! And remember: The vast majority of job openings are never advertised—they're filled by word of mouth.

Unfortunately, many job seekers are hesitant to network because they're afraid of seeming pushy, annoying or self-serving. But networking isn't about using other people or aggressively promoting yourself—it's about building relationships. As you look for a new job, these relationships can provide much-needed feedback, advice and support.

Strongly consider joining professional industry associations, career transition groups and special interest groups. Get involved in community projects, volunteer work, anything that speaks to your interests. Know that the person you will be in five years is determined, in part, by the people you meet and the relationships you develop between now and then.

TIM

I work in book publishing, an industry that is going through some big transformations due to technological changes and the consolidation of media companies. This has led to a significant amount of job loss in the industry—including my own position, when the department I worked in at a big publishing house was cut by 50 percent.

At first I thought that my layoff couldn't have come at a worse time. My wife and I had a four year old and were a two-income household, I was dealing with a number of family issues that needed to be resolved and, of course, the job market and economy were in a tailspin.

But the benefit of hindsight allowed me to see that the time off was a blessing. I was able to assist my mom as her health declined, I spent real quality time with my family and got back to being more involved in my community. We also learned to live on a smaller income and take enjoyment in things that are free and adjust our lifestyle accordingly.

When I was working at the big publishing company, I had more than a two-hour commute by train every day. That meant I was waking up at 5 a.m. to get in to the office by 8 a.m. so that I could leave by 5 p.m. to catch a train back. This would get me home around 7:30 p.m. It was a long day. I felt like I never saw my son awake. My wife was like a single parent, and my dog lost interest in playing Frisbee. (Well, in all honesty, it was probably me who was too tired to play Frisbee. I shouldn't blame the dog. He's a loyal friend.)

After my layoff I was a "Mr. Mom" and really enjoyed it. The house was incredibly clean, I learned to cook and bake and I finally got to all of those projects that had been on my "to-do" list. One of the best things I did early on was to join my local gym. I would get to the gym at about 5:30 a.m. every morning and work out. Over three to four months, I lost the 20 extra pounds that I had gained during my long days of commuting, and it was a great stress release from the job search tensions.

After getting back from the gym, I would make breakfast for my son and wife and pack a lunch for him. After the bus picked him up, I would spend the day calling and contacting potential leads and sending out letters and emails. I tried to stick to a schedule to stay focused.

During my job hunt, I searched the usual websites (Monster, Career Builder, Linked-In, etc.), as well as the websites specific to my industry, on a daily basis. When I saw an appropriate position, I would send a cover letter and résumé, but I only ever secured interviews with about 20 to 25 percent of them. I had more success working with head hunters. There are several agencies that specialize in my industry, and they were very good about getting me interviews for specific positions. I also networked and contacted previous colleagues and friends at other companies.

And I turned to books. As I said, I work in publishing, and my wife is a librarian, so our house is full of them. Some of the books I found useful for keeping a positive attitude as I went through that job-loss transition included *No Job, No Prob,* about how to make the most of your time off during a job change; *Great Failures of the Highly Successful*—as the title implies, it is a collection of stories about famous people and how they dealt with and overcame adversity; and *100 Simple Secrets of Happy People* and *100 Simple Secrets of Successful People.*

After six long months of interviewing and pursuing many leads, I eventually received several offers. I ended up choosing not the highest-paying job or the one that was the most prestigious, but rather a small start-up company with great potential. It was a difficult decision, since two of the other offers were much closer to my previous positions. But I have been in the position for a while now, and I feel that I made the right choice. I enjoy my job, and business is growing rapidly. I am still able to have the work/life balance that I had during my layoff. My dog is happier than ever.

I also take great pleasure in helping other friends and colleagues with their job searches and letting them know that there is a light at the end of the tunnel.

AUTHOR ANONYMOUS
at the writer's request.

CHAPTER 8
BE STILL—PRACTICE MINDFULNESS

"Surrender to what is. Let go of what was. Have faith in what will be." —Sonia Ricotti

Jon Kabat-Zinn, Professor of Medicine Emeritus and creator of the Stress Reduction Clinic and the Center for Mindfulness in Medicine, Health Care, and Society at the University of Massachusetts Medical School, describes mindfulness as the act of paying attention in a particular way, on purpose, in the present moment, non-judgmentally.

There have been lots of articles and media attention devoted to mindfulness in the last few years. One reason is that the number of studies being conducted on the benefits of mindfulness has exploded. We now have evidence that developing a mindfulness practice can improve your mood and sense of well-being (*Journal of Religion and Health*, June 2014), can regulate mood and anxiety disorders (*JAMA Internal Medicine*, 2014) and reduces the likelihood of depression in adolescents (ScienceDaily, March 2013). Many of the studies on the benefits of mindfulness have shown results in just a few short weeks.

Meditation is one of the key components of practicing mindfulness. It is quite simple, although not always easy. It takes discipline and the ability and willingness to be present with your thoughts and feelings. And, incidentally, mindfulness can be practiced anytime, anywhere, for any length of time. Try it while you're taking the dog out for a walk, you're on hold with customer service, during your shower or bath (my personal favorite), just as you awake in the morning or before sleep in the evening. The opportunities are limitless. Developing a mindfulness practice can be one of your most powerful tools for navigating through the experience of job loss, and it can help you find your way through to the other side.

CAROL

When my job as Vice President of Project Management and Training for a national nonprofit organization in southern California ended, I wasn't too concerned...at first. I'd spent the previous 20 years successfully working my way up the corporate ladder. I knew it would be a challenge, but I had no doubt that I would land another great job in a few short months.

I had gotten a job right out of high school with a large bank. Through hard work and experience, I advanced quickly. I was successful at every opportunity that came my way. However, at one point I hit a brick wall because I had no college education.

For years, I lamented the fact that I had blown off college as a young adult. I began toying with the idea of getting my education even though I was now 36 years old. Could I do it? The answer was clear; I made the decision to enroll in college and obtain my bachelor's degree. It was hard, but I found juggling a career, children and college a challenge I thoroughly enjoyed. In fours years, I graduated with honors.

There was no goal too big, so I took my experience and education and landed some prestigious jobs. Rather than just being the top in my department, now I held positions such as director of operations and vice president at different companies. I held the titles and enjoyed the money that came with them. I worked hard, I paid my dues, I was finally at the top. But it was more than the amount of money I made—it was the symbol of how much I was worth that I clung to.

It all came crashing down in a moment. With the country in an economic crisis, I was suddenly unemployed and faced with the task of finding a new job. For the first time in my working life, I felt lost. Now that I wasn't working 10- to 12-hour days, I actually had time to chat with people I hadn't talked to in months or even years. An old friend asked me how I'd tackled my job searches in the past. I simply replied, "I've never had to look for a job. They always just land in my lap."

Not wanting to be idle, I decided to write a book that I had been thinking about for years. When I wasn't writing, I applied for jobs that seemed to be a fit, I networked, I called old employers and friends. When I wasn't tackling the seemingly impossible job search, I wrote, I cried and I prayed.

More than 13 months later, the book in near-publishable format, I found myself still unemployed and deeply depressed. Getting out of bed and attempting to do anything productive became a challenge. There were days when I did absolutely nothing. I was forced to face a very difficult truth about myself. I had wrapped up my whole identity and self-worth in my career and my dollar value as a corporate executive.

Now that my "career" was gone, I felt completely worthless as a person. I searched my soul for answers and God began doing a new work in my life. I was forced to depend on my faith alone because I could not see where I was headed.

As I built a new foundation for life and work, I sought a new direction. My sights were no longer on the hard, cold corporate ladder but on level ground, where I could clearly see people in need all around me.

Rather than seeking out a company that could do things for me financially and boost my ego, I took a deep look within myself. I found the inner strengths and talents that could be transferred to serving humanity instead of a company. I truly desired to become a person with a servant's heart.

Once I let go of the old me, God landed me in the perfect place. He brought me a local rescue mission to serve the homeless in my community. Every day I was overwhelmed by the miracles I saw with the men, women and children I helped. Lives were truly changed with a little hope, guidance and God's love. I spent a couple of years getting myself grounded by working with the least, the last and the lost. I "found myself" there. My book was published, and it was no coincidence that the topic of the book is finding hope when life hurts.

Ultimately I went back to the corporate world, but I took on a position with a global organization to manage their corporate social responsibility programs and charity work. The big title did not need to be a part of my work. I find I now work hard to make a positive difference in the world, not because of who I work for or what they pay me, but because of who I am.

Taking my ego out of the equation and adding God's direction was the solution to my problem. I may never be rich, but I am truly blessed. I have a new résumé, a résumé of self-worth. Not written by me, but written by the Master.

ABOUT CAROL E. URTON:

Sharing the message of hope, healing, salvation, and forgiveness. If you have ever wondered where God is amidst the trials we all face in life, you will want to read Carol's book, *When Hope Hurts.*

Carol is an accomplished writer and speaker whose goal is to inspire people to achieve their full potential despite hardships in life. She is passionate about issues relating to childhood abuse and neglect. Carol is also known nationally for her work with Web Wise Kids, speaking on the topic of Internet safety helping youth and adults understand how to have a safe and positive experience while online, social networking and using cell phones.

If you need a memorable speaker with passion, content-rich material and experience, contact Carol at carolurton@gmail.com or www.findinghopeministries.com.

CHAPTER 9
TAKE CONTROL OF
YOUR HABITS

"Take control of your habits, take control of your life."
—Success Begins Today

During the time following your layoff, it is critical to maintain healthy habits and take excellent care of yourself. You now have the time to exercise, get outdoors and enjoy physical activities that you were not able to slot in while working all day! Move your body on a daily basis, as this profoundly impacts your mood and emotions. Set a small goal for yourself, every day, and keep track of your progress. Eat regular, healthy meals and avoid heavy drinking. Get plenty of sleep.

Taking the steps to support and nurture your body, mind and soul will decrease your anxiety and stress. Read inspirational articles or stories, or anything that makes you feel good. Reach out to friends and family members who make you laugh or who are really upbeat. To encourage a positive frame of mind, it is important to surround yourself with just that: positivity. Your actions and habits help define who you are.

SARAH

Following 12 years working in both retail and business-to-business sales, I began working for a consumer electronics manufacturer in the field merchandising division of sales. I loved the flexible schedule, no sales quotas and the interaction with retailers, and I believed in the product I was representing. I excelled at this position, finishing projects ahead of time, training and promoting the product with retailers and winning national awards for special events and branding at retail.

After seven years as a field merchandiser, I was promoted to an assistant district manager position. This position allowed me to mentor other field merchandising reps and also assist my district and regional managers. Within a year, my regional manager began talking with me about promoting me to a district manager, and that happened several months later.

My career as a district manager was very rewarding. During my eight years in this role I managed between eight and 10 reps at any given time in six states. I did my job well and earned "exceeds expectations" on my annual performance reviews. The organization supported education for its employees, and I took advantage of this. I enrolled in many computer application courses and joined Toastmasters in an effort to improve my communication and leadership skills. As a manager, I motivated a high-performing team. Many of the reps in my district were chosen for special projects and national events. I loved my job and enjoyed working and communicating with my direct reports and my regional manager. I planned on working in this capacity and this organization until I retired.

Shortly after the company recognized my 16th anniversary in 2012, my position—along with another district manager role, two regional manager roles and an administrative staff position—was eliminated during fiscal year budget cuts. Although the subsidiary I worked for was profitable, other subsidiaries in the corporation had suffered billions of dollars in losses, and the parent corporation directed each subsidiary to make equal reductions in staff. I knew that other subsidiaries had had losses, but I didn't anticipate that it would impact me personally. But the moment I received an invitation to meet with the director in my local market, I realized that I could potentially be laid off. I prepared for the worst and sought advice from colleagues prior to the meeting.

The meeting was brief: I was given a severance package, my equipment was disabled and I received instructions not to contact anyone in the organization other than HR.

I was furious! And devastated. I took it very personally and couldn't see it as a business measure. I was very insecure about launching a job search at 53. I hadn't conducted a job search in nearly 17 years. The company had just recognized my tenure of 16 years and then eliminated my position—they didn't allow me to step down, and they didn't offer me any other employment options.

Losing a job when you've worked for the company for more than 15 years is like finding out that you have cancer or getting divorced. I'd worked with many of my colleagues for 10 or more years, and we didn't want to be separated. Perhaps the hardest part of my termination was not being able to manage or support my direct reports anymore. I continued to stay in touch with many of them and still am, even more than three years later.

Change is hard for everyone. To have that amount of change happen to me so abruptly was very hard and confusing. I felt pressure to find a job quickly so that I could keep contributing to our two-family income.

I received a generous severance check, immediately filed for unemployment and began taking advantage of the transition services my former employer provided to remarket myself. Within a week of my layoff I'd started looking for a job. I also went through a variety of emotions during those first few weeks: anger, sadness, fear, regret, relief, hope. My stress level, thankfully, was relatively low.

Through the transition organization, I met other people about the same age as me with similar stories, some with much higher salary losses than mine. I updated my résumé and learned new techniques and resources for job searches. I connected with former employees from my past sales career. I networked with people within the Toastmasters organization. I marketed myself and made hundreds of connections on social media through Linked In.

Before long, I started feeling hopeful. I committed to taking on a one-year leadership role within the Toastmasters organization, serving as president of my local club and area governor for five additional clubs. I also joined Weight Watchers and lost 30 pounds and started gaining confidence.

As I searched for my next career, I challenged myself and my leadership abilities. My interview skills improved. During that first year I had several job opportunities and worked for a few companies, none of which fulfilled my expectations or compared to the job I had lost, but they paid more than unemployment and allowed me to contribute to the household.

One of my former colleagues who had also lost his job ended up working for another consumer products manufacturer. We had several conversations that led up to me joining him a few months later. Two years later, I'm still there, working in an industry where I thrive best.

My current position is as a field marketing representative for a manufacturer of consumer goods. Although I'm not managing people, I am managing accounts in two major cities in two adjoining states and travel frequently between the two cities to support the more than 400 retail doors.

I look back on what happened to me three years ago as one of my best life experiences and the most challenging time of my career. My only regret is that I should have been more selective in my job search during the first year, and taken some time to enjoy not working! In the end, the experience led me to exactly where I should be and helped me recognize my strengths as well as my weaknesses. I'm stronger and wiser because of losing my job.

AUTHOR ANONYMOUS
at the writer's request.

SUSAN

I live in the small town of Millbury, Massachusetts. In 1977 I accepted a full-time job as a tax assistant for a local insurance company, embarking on a long-term career and dedicating myself to that business. In 1980, with an incentive of tuition reimbursement, I enrolled in community college and began taking classes toward a degree. At work, I was recognized several times for my administrative efforts.

I continued school and in 1987, I graduated from an associate's program. Due to health reasons, I began part-time hours in 1989. The company merged with another carrier in 1992, and the two tax departments were combined. At that time, I eagerly accepted an opportunity for a more thought-provoking role. My new supervisor was a great mentor, and she helped me become a fine insurance tax professional.

Later, the company demutualized and went through a name change. It was leadership's plan to eventually go public, which soon meant still another name change. The internal climate began to shift, and the organization experienced numerous shake-ups.

I survived several rounds of layoffs. My supervisor left for personal reasons, so I gained a new boss. In 2005, I was asked to consider continuing my education. After some thought, I agreed to pursue a bachelor's in accounting. Over the span of several years, I took online classes. At times, my classes were demanding and frustrating, but I persisted and finally secured my degree in 2011. Meanwhile, I continued being acknowledged for my successes at work and receiving promotions. By now, the company was involved in several mergers and acquisitions. The tax department was shrinking, but the workload was increasing.

In May of 2011 I learned that my position—and five others in finance—was being eliminated. The state tax accounting and compliance work that I did was being transferred overseas to India. This news was disheartening to say the least. I had been employed by this insurance company for nearly 34 years. The first days without my job were awkward. Reality soon set in, and it was clear that I did not have the luxury of staying home. There were people who told me that I should relax and enjoy the free time, but I could not let my guard down. I wanted to remain focused, and so I began serious pursuit of employment. I constructed a new résumé with the help of outplacement services and attended workshops and filed for benefits with the assistance of a local career center.

Just two weeks after my dismissal I was struck with yet another blow when test results confirmed that I had bladder cancer. The urologist was surprised, but expressed the fortune of having caught it early. Within a month, I underwent surgery to remove the small tumor. The results of subsequent cystoscopies have thankfully been normal.

Initially, in my job hunt, I expected to find an accounting position with comparable salary. I had recently earned an undergraduate degree and considered my accounting background, computer literacy and other soft skills to be transferrable. Much to my dismay, I was told by one particular recruiter that my experience was much too specific in one industry. Nevertheless, I continued to press on. Whenever I interviewed, I would take time afterward to write notes on the exchange. I networked with friends, relatives, neighbors and former colleagues with hopes of generating job leads. I kept building my LinkedIn connections and participating in group discussions. That is where I crossed paths with the author of this book who was writing a very influential story. I agreed to help her.

While unemployed, I tried to adhere to a daily routine so that I could stay productive, and did whatever it took to stay energized. I liked being available for my family, planning new meals, and doing whatever I could to make the household run smoothly. However, that did not pay the bills. All I wanted was a steady paycheck, but I knew that I would have to adapt to the idea of radically reduced wages. In my mind, being employed was better than no job at all. I networked via LinkedIn, communicated with friends and continued to tell my story to anyone who was willing to listen.

It was also important to me to decompress regularly, and I still find walking to be stimulating and reflective. My family has always had my back, and I knew their love and support would help me to overcome these traumatic events. I have been married to my husband for more than 30 years and we have two grown children. My mom and sister live nearby.

My husband and I found it necessary to do some belt-tightening. He had taken early retirement from his job as town mechanic, and his pension provided a deeply decreased percentage of his salary, so I had anxiety about making ends meet once my benefits expired. In retirement he took charge of the town's paid-call fire department, and the money he earns as chief further helps to pay our bills. As an active member of the Millbury Fire Department Ladies Auxiliary, I connect with the community through this channel, too, and our group frequently conducts various fundraising events.

It is a proven fact that a majority of job seekers find work through a personal or professional contact. Many times it is who you know.

It is also said that as one door closes, another opens. For me, this proved true. In December 2012, the week following receipt of my last benefits check, I was offered a position as a customer service representative for a local oil company. I worked there until May 2014, when my boss downsized the office for the summer and I was laid off for a second time. I fully expected to be called back in the fall, but that did not happen. Again, I was hitting the pavement.

Sometime during my second job search, I became emotionally disconnected. I felt as though I was squandering my time if I was on Facebook or doing something frivolous. As days turned to weeks, and weeks turned to months, my confidence decreased and my anxiety rose. When I realized that what I was doing was not effective, the longer I kept doing it, the worse I felt. But I am a firm believer that everything happens for a reason and that good things do come to those who wait. To those who find themselves in a similar situation, I would say, Keep checking job postings, remain diligent in networking, consider volunteer work, learn new skills and do whatever it takes to remain positive.

Somewhere inside me I found the spiritual inspiration to move on to better things. It was not only the realization that I had to work but that I truly felt the need for structure in my life. When all was said and done, I learned that redefining oneself is an overwhelming task, especially following long-term employment. I was proactive about learning new skills, and those skills helped me land my next and current role as a customer service representative for a local insurance agency.

All these experiences have shown me that job loss can be humbling. The road map of life is prone to changes and there are no guarantees. Without a doubt, these experiences and events of the past few years have made me stronger. I have faith in God and my belief is that He never gives us more than we can bear.

AUTHOR ANONYMOUS
at the writer's request.

CHAPTER 10
BE A SURVIVOR

"You are not a victim, you are a victor." —Joel Osteen

One of the biggest challenges of unemployment can be managing your emotions so that you don't see yourself as a victim (for very long). While it's important to acknowledge how difficult job loss and unemployment can be, it's equally important to avoid wallowing, and to stay connected to a sense of possibility about your future. Rather than dwelling on your job loss—how unfair it is, how poorly it was handled, things you could have done to prevent it, how much better life would be if it hadn't happened—try to accept the situation. The sooner you do, the sooner you can get on with the next phase of your life. Feel strong, confident and excited for your future, and your future will not disappoint you.

ANGELA

My story begins in the summer of 1989—for me, the summer between high school and college. It was also the summer the movie *Dead Poets Society* was released, and I saw it in the theater five times.

I was a terrible student and only liked the social aspects of school. My grade point average was so low that any state college would have laughed at my application. My friends had all been accepted at various universities, and I was already mourning the loss of my social life. At the last minute I decided to attend a community college and major in broadcasting, at the urging of friends who feared I'd do nothing. I'd worked for our high school TV station for two years and broadcasting was something I excelled at, but it didn't ignite passion in me.

I had always loved literature and writing. I'd been writing poems and short stories since the age of 10. Eight English credits were needed to graduate from my high school; I graduated with 12, taking every English class I could. So when I saw *Dead Poets Society* for the first time, I felt a fire light up inside me. Robin Williams's character, John Keating, is a new English teacher at an all-boys preparatory school in 1959 New England. He encourages his students to use literature and poetry as muses for their lives and inspires them to find their own creativity and "swim against the stream." Keating empowers his students to express what's in their hearts and minds, and the movie's key message—"carpe diem," Latin for "seize the day"—became a beautiful reminder to live each day as if it were my last.

In my favorite scene, Keating tells his students to create their own funny walk to set themselves apart. As the majority of them are walking around the courtyard, laughing, one student, Charlie Dalton, stays still. Keating, noticing, addresses him, "Will you be joining us, Charlie?" Charlie responds, "Demonstrating the right *not* to walk." Keating nods his head knowingly and says, "Thank you, Mr. Dalton. You've just illustrated the point." Every time I watched that scene I felt my inner rebel respond. I was desperate to be someone other than who I was. I wanted to be creative, fearless and inspiring.

I wish I could say that *Dead Poets Society* enabled me to strike out and become a revolutionary. It did not. But it did inspire me to switch my major to English. Once I graduated I was all over the map—I worked for an insurance company, mutual funds and in private education, and finally landed in publishing.

I was fortunate enough to be hired as an editor's assistant for a national travel magazine and learned a lot from my colleagues. I did so well that I became assistant editor for the magazine a year later. I'd written and edited for years as an English major, but this was journalism-style writing and it was very appealing. Unfortunately, in 2000, after two years on the job, the company hired a new CEO, and the ensuing organizational housecleaning landed me on the street.

I was devastated. It was the first time I'd ever been let go from a job, and I internalized the anguish. Sure, I'd made some mistakes in the job, but I didn't deserve to be downsized. Desperate for work, within a month I accepted a position at another large corporation, my first job in marketing. After working for a travel magazine with padded deadlines, I didn't comprehend the immediacy of marketing at first, and I honestly didn't know what the hell I was doing. Writing copy in 20 minutes? Routing a project through the art and editorial departments in record time? It all seemed very strange to me. Actually, it still does.

After my three-month probationary period, I was fired. This firing was within five months of my first job loss. I felt like the lowest of the low. Why couldn't I just fit into the corporate structure? I saw my friends excelling at their jobs and wondered what was wrong with me. Between jobs I relied on my writing and editing capabilities to land freelance work. Many former colleagues believed in my abilities, even when I didn't.

In January 2001, I was hired by an international service organization to prepare their materials for print and web. My boss thought I was the best thing since sliced bread, until I questioned the process of a few projects and became friends with the department's administrative assistant, who was not well-liked by our boss. It was guilt by association, and my boss began disliking both of us. Within six months, the organization hired Arthur Andersen as consultants. By the end of September, my job was magically eliminated—my third firing in less than two years.

Looking back, I can see that I ignored all the signs that working for someone else was not for me. But at the time I just internalized all the job loss and felt stupid and worthless, and I wasn't ready yet to strike out on my own.

I took another job, this one in marketing and public relations at an art museum. For the first time I had a boss who really encouraged me and believed in me, which was wonderful. I gained back some much-needed confidence, but the pay was terrible. My dream job, or so I thought, in marketing opened at another museum in town. I'd heard horrible things about the organization, but I threw myself headlong into the job. After just two weeks, I knew I'd made a terrible mistake. I felt trapped.

This was the first time that deep depression reared its ugly head. I hated going to work and would cry in my car on the way there. I was drained. I had no energy. I felt insignificant and sad. I hung in as long as I could. When my boss spoke with me about creating a performance improvement plan, I admitted that I knew I wasn't being a team player, but I still couldn't seem to care. Things got so bad that I contemplated suicide. Finally, in July 2004, one year and one week after I'd accepted the position, I was fired.

I felt immense pain and humiliation, but strangely, I also felt free. A friend did his best to bolster me with confidence, comparing me to a revolutionary—I didn't fit anywhere, he said, because I was meant to stand out and make a difference. I tried to buy into it, but I still felt wounded. I'd been fired four times in four years. And yet I also felt so relieved.

In February 2005, a friend recommended me for a public relations manager position with a state agency. My new boss thought I walked on water. I loved my position. I traveled the state. I planned press conferences for high-ranking officials and even spoke to Oprah Winfrey's producers about doing a segment. I loved my coworkers. I loved my boss. I did everything I could to make the agency look good to the public. I'm still unsure exactly what happened during my tenure there, and I joke with my friends that my name should be Lucifer because I began as a beloved angel and fell from grace, but in May 2006 I was fired. I felt defeat, but again liberation, and this time the feeling of freedom was much stronger. I felt enlightened by this firing, but didn't yet know how.

My freelance public and media relations work flourished, but I mistook my talent for passion. I truly thought that this work was my contribution to the world. But it wasn't. I'd read authors such as Dr. Wayne Dyer, SARK,

Louise Hays, Martha Beck and Anthony Robbins and I was always invigorated by their words. They talked of the same things that John Keating did in *Dead Poets Society*: Be your own person. Make your mark. Be passionate. Find what you love, and the money will follow. I swallowed these words like a hungry child, but I never truly believed them. I always thought these messages were for other people, not me. I had credit card debt, a mortgage, car payments and no hope for a truly bright future. I couldn't afford to just find what I loved and hope the money would follow. I lacked confidence and a view of the big picture.

Over the years I continued experiencing bouts of depression and anxiety, but never dealt with it effectively. I would go on medication for a while and then go off. Looking back now, I can see that I clearly needed help and didn't ask for it. Every time I was reprimanded for something, even if it wasn't my fault, I felt ashamed and worthless. Other people I knew were able to stay in jobs for years and never seemed as restless as me. Why couldn't I do that? What the hell was wrong with me?

Finally, at 42, I decided I needed to challenge myself to take on a corporate marketing position and rise through the ranks. I convinced myself that I'd just never stuck it out long enough in a job and that I could do it this time. I took a job with a very large corporation that managed car auctions all over North America. My boss loved me. My boss's boss loved me. I was on a fast track to success. I could multitask with the best of them and turn a project around in a heartbeat. It seemed that I'd actually gotten my shit together and was succeeding.

While I was working there, my husband and I bought a new home. It is a gorgeous home and everything I've ever wanted. I will always be grateful that the job helped us qualify for our mortgage. My joy about the house didn't last, though. Within two months, my depression came back with a vengeance. Work did nothing but frustrate me and make me question my existence. A reorganization of the marketing department meant I lost my wonderful boss and was forced to report to a manager in another state. Many times, I found out department news before she did. The set up was poorly constructed. As many as 30 projects came across my desk in a day's time. I tried to maintain everything as best I could, but the depression was winning. I began getting migraines and being dizzy and irritable. I would cry on the way to work and cry on the way home. I kept telling myself, "One foot in front of the other," but I felt myself slipping down the rabbit hole.

I'd been spending weeks in tears and wishing I could disappear. I didn't want to do things that made me happy. I put on a façade every day for my coworkers, friends and family. I looked at suicidal tendency checklists, and I met all of the criteria. I stayed home sick one day and asked my husband to take the dog to doggie daycare. I wanted the day to myself to cry on the couch, and I was determined to call the city crisis line for help. It took everything in me to call them. The gentleman who answered was kind and compassionate. He suggested I see my psychiatrist or go to the stress center, but warned me that it was sometimes tough to get into the stress center because they only have so many beds. I cried and cried until my husband came home. He admitted to me that he was worried that he might come home to me dead. I made an appointment with my psychiatrist. She gave me prescriptions for meds, but they wouldn't really kick in for a few weeks. I tried to put on a mask so that I didn't have to admit to her how bad it really was.

No one at work had the slightest suspicion of what I was going through. I hid it very well. But at one point it hit me that while the depression was very real, the job had been its catalyst. And all I could think about was having it be over. On Friday, May 17, 2013, I cleared all personal files, e-mails and superfluous items from my computer and desk. I made a list of priorities on a notebook page and placed it on top of my work pile. To the inexperienced eye, it looked like I'd just organized my desk and made a list of things to do on Monday. The truth was that I was cleaning things out and making it easy for someone else to take over my workload on Monday. I thought it likely that I would kill myself over the weekend.

I somehow made it back to work on Monday, and at lunch I verbally vomited all over my closest co-worker, telling her everything. She was shocked. She told me to call my boss (in another state, remember) and tell her I was sick and needed to go home. She told me to call my husband and have him take me to the stress center immediately. She said she would work with my husband to take care of any issues at work. I will always credit her with helping to save my life.

I spent three days in the stress center and did outpatient therapy for the duration of the summer. It finally occurred to me that my depression really *was* that bad, and I was determined to get help. I felt so much better after just a few weeks, and I realized that the job quite literally nearly killed me.

I'd had 15 jobs in 20 years. I could say that everything bad that's happened to me in my career has been at the hands of others, but the fact is, I chose those roles. I chose to work for those organizations, and I chose my actions at each place. Sure, there were shitty micromanaging bosses, backstabbing coworkers and thankless hours spent working special events, but I recognize my place in these situations. And I've realized that all those firings were part of what made me who I am today.

In July 2013, with the support and love of my husband, I made the choice to pursue a new career path. It was time to find my purpose and passion, not just another job. I had come too close to losing my life to risk that happening again. I began meeting with a life coach who helped me identify my passions, talents and values. I'd always been intrigued by counseling and coaching, but didn't know how to channel that interest. By November I'd enrolled in a coaching program and begun my training. The instructors emphasized that nothing is truly a mistake. Our experiences shape us into who we are. I felt energized, and it finally hit me: I was home. I was with people who spoke my language, and my purpose had a name—life coach.

Now I help others who struggle in their jobs to find their true happiness. I help people "reset their happy." And I've never looked back. Losing job after job was the best thing that's ever happened to me. I developed resilience and strength. All those firings were building blocks for my future, and I use all my experiences to propel myself forward.

I wish that I'd become a coach sooner, but I can honestly say that it took everything I went through to get me here. Losing jobs wasn't the jumping off point for my life, it was what catapulted me into my new life.

As John Keating always said, "Carpe diem."

ABOUT ANGELA JORDEN:

Angela Jorden is a life and career coach who loves to see the transformations that clients make when they are empowered and championed. She works with mid-career professionals who are ready to exchange their corporate jobs for a life of fulfillment and purpose. She is a proud Hoosier who resides in Indianapolis, Indiana, with her husband, two dogs and cat. www.resetyourhappy.com

APPENDICES
CAREER TRANSITION COACHING QUESTIONS

Thought-provoking coaching questions are just one of the many tools used by professional coaches. Coaching questions are not presented to elicit more information from the client but rather to provoke the client to think, feel or react differently about the issue at hand.

The following list of questions was kindly contributed by Jennifer Barley. As the KickStart Coach, Jenn helps clients get inspired and get in the game through the use of coaching questions. Use these questions as you move forward on your journey to help you identify your calling, purpose and areas of interest in your career.

- If you could make a living doing anything in the world, regardless of any constraints, what would you do?

- What about that career is appealing to you?

- What is it that is driving you to change your current situation?

- What parts of your job do you enjoy?

- What parts of your job do you dislike?

- What are your strengths at work?

- When do you feel your best at work?

- When do you feel you are not at your best at work?

- What is the current payoff for being in your work environment?

- In what ways do you sabotage yourself at your current job?

- Where do you limit yourself at work?

- What changes could you make to have a more fulfilling work life?

- In what ways does your current work environment support your motivation at work?

- What skills do you need to develop to have the greatest impact in your current job?

- What opportunities do you see in your current career?

- Who are you in relation to your job?

- What do you love to do for hobbies?

- What are your favorite books and magazines?

- Where have you been successful in your life?

- Describe the last time you felt you were authentic and expressed yourself fully?

- What are your top three talents?

- What were your favorite classes in high school or college?

- What is your life purpose?

- How can you link together your life purpose and earning a living?

- How does your work reflect your top values?

- What information do you want to gather to learn more about possibilities?

- In what ways do you want to explore your desired new field?

- What are the benefits of changing careers?

- Who do you want to BE in your career?

- What type of work are you passionate about?

- What steps do you need to take to explore your new career?

- What is stopping you from having the career you have always dreamed of?

- When you think of the optimal workplace, what comes to mind?

- How would you begin your day?

- What would you be doing throughout the day?

- What types of people do you love working with?

- How is the workplace environment?

- What benefits are important to you? (then rank in order)

For more information on Jennifer Barley, The KickStart Coach®, go to www.jenniferbarley.com.

THE BENEFITS OF DAILY AFFIRMATIONS

"What we think, we become." —Buddha

I'm a huge fan of affirmations. I believe they help define your focus. And defining your focus is the best first step when you're trying to accomplish any goal.

Affirmations help to generate creativity, and, if you involve a spiritual element, they can even help to inspire real blessings. I mix my affirmations with prayer, and I can't count the number of times I've begun doing that and have seen my goals come to pass shortly thereafter. You can literally begin to feel a shift into possibility when you begin affirming.

Other benefits of affirmations include:

- You become aware of your daily thoughts and words, reducing the risk of letting negativity seep in.

- You notice more synchronicities in your life, which serves to encourage and motivate you to keep up the practice.

- Daily affirmations not only help keep you surrounded by the things you want in your life but they help bring about more blessings and gifts.

- A daily practice helps to keep the small things in perspective. In this high-speed world you can easily lose sight of how large the small things really are. When healthy, you may forget to think of how much you appreciate it. A simple morning affirmation sentence of "I am healthy" can go a long way.

- A recent study shows that optimistic people have healthier hearts, and affirmations help you to stay positive.

- As you continue this practice, others take note and you begin to help those around you without even trying. This, in turn, helps keep you focused.

- Daily affirmations keep you in a constant state of gratitude.

Here are some of my favorite affirmations from the Living With the Law of Attraction program with Katherine Hurst. And, if you're on Facebook, be sure to follow John Assaraf's page (www.facebook.com/johnassarafpage) as he posts wonderful affirmations daily.

- Today is a new day.

- Today I begin to create a new life of incredible abundance and joy.

- Today is the day that I decide to take action and discover the secrets of living the life I love.

- Today I choose to release all negativity and the mistakes of my past.

- I can change my life.

- I am ready to take charge of my happiness.

- I am master of my own destiny.

- I can have, be or choose anything I choose.

- I celebrate my power as creator of my life.

- I will do whatever it takes to achieve my goals.

- I am transforming into the person I want to be.

- I have complete belief in myself that I am transforming my life.

- I am safe to let go of the past and look forward to an exciting new future.

- Nothing but positive things await me, and I know things are exactly as they should be.

- There are no limits in what I can manifest in my life.

- Positive thoughts come naturally to me.

- I am free to make my life anything that I want it to be.

- My will to learn and to succeed is growing stronger every day.

- My life is full of miracles.

- I am creating a wonderful future for myself right now.

- I recognize that every moment is a new opportunity to start again.

- I am moving closer to my dreams every day.

- I seek to be the best and grow more successful each day.

- The power that has created me is the same power I use to create my life.

- My positive energy draws new positive circumstances, opportunities and people into my life every day.

RESOURCES

As I mentioned in Chapter 6, "Learn Something New Every Day", after I lost my job(s), I immersed myself in personal-development and educational books, workshops and retreats. And, as you know from the rest of the stories you read, I was not the only one. For your benefit, here's a roundup of books, virtual learning programs and organizations that helped us and so many others gain clarity and perspective on our career transitions. I hope they help you, too.

BOOKS (IN ALPHABETICAL ORDER)

- *7 Strategies for Wealth & Happiness: Power Ideas from America's Foremost Business Philosopher,* by Jim Rohn

- *The 100 Simple Secrets of Happy People: What Scientists Have Learned and How You Can Use It,* by David Niven, PhD

- *100 Simple Secrets of Successful People, The: What Scientists Have Learned and How You Can Use It,* by David Niven, PhD

- *A Course in Miracles,* by Dr. Helen Schucman

- *A Thousand Names for Joy: Living in Harmony with the Way Things Are,* by Byron Katie and Stephen Mitchell

- *Awaken the Giant Within: How to Take Immediate Control of Your Mental, Emotional, Physical and Financial Destiny,* by Tony Robbins

- *Break Out!: 5 Keys to Go Beyond Your Barriers and Live an Extraordinary Life,* by Joel Osteen

- *Chicken Soup for the Soul: Reboot Your Life—101 Stories about Finding a New Path to Happiness,* by Amy Newmark and Claire Cook

- *Choosing Hope: Moving Forward from Life's Darkest Hours,* by Kaitlin Roig-DeBellis and Robin Gaby Fisher

- *Daring Greatly: How the Courage to Be Vulnerable Transforms the Way We Live, Love, Parent, and Lead,* by Brené Brown

- *Drive: The Surprising Truth About What Motivates Us,* by Daniel H. Pink

- *Energy Leadership: Transforming Your Workplace and Your Life from the Core,* by Bruce D. Schneider

- *Healing After Job Loss: 100 Practical Ideas,* by Alan D. Wolfelt PhD and Kirby J. Duvall MD (part of the "Healing Your Grieving Heart" series)

- *Heroes Get Hired: How To Use Your Military Experience to Master the Interview,* by Michelle Tillis Lederman and Col. Jack Jacobs (Ret.)

- *How Successful People Think: Change Your Thinking, Change Your Life*, by John C. Maxwell

- *I Can See Clearly Now*, by Dr. Wayne W. Dyer

- *Life Makeovers: 52 Practical & Inspiring Ways to Improve Your Life One Week at a Time*, by Cheryl Richardson

- *Living Your Best Year Ever*, by Darren Hardy

- *Make Job Loss Work for You: Get Over It and Get Your Career Back On Track*, by Richard Deems and Terri Deems

- *Mindfulness: An Eight-Week Plan for Finding Peace in a Frantic World*, by Mark Williams and Danny Penman

- *Moving On: New Life After Job Loss—A Guide to Picking Yourself Up, Shaking Off the Dirt, and Getting On With Your Life*, by Paul C. Larsen

- *Nail the Interview, Land the Job: A Step-by-Step Guide for What to Do Before, During, and After the Interview*, by Michelle Tillis Lederman

- *No Job? No Prob!: How to Pay Your Bills, Feed Your Mind, and Have a Blast When You're Out of Work* by Nicholas Nigro

- *O's Little Book of Happiness*, by Oprah Winfrey and O, The Oprah Magazine

- *Overcoming Redundancy: 52 Inspiring Ideas to Help You Bounce Back from Losing Your Job*, by Gordon Adams

- *Parting Company: How to Survive the Loss of a Job and Find Another Successfully,* by William J. Morin and James C. Cabrera

- *Peaks and Valleys: Making Good and Bad Times Work for You—At Work and in Life,* by Spencer Johnson M.D.

- *Reboot Your Life: Energize Your Career and Life by Taking a Break,* by Catherine Allen and Nancy Bearg

- *Rebound: A Proven Plan for Starting Over After Job Loss,* by Martha I. Finney

- *Reinvent Yourself: A Lesson in Personal Leadership,* by John J. Murphy

- *Reset: How to Beat the Job-Loss Blues and Get Ready for Your Next Act,* by Dwain Schenck

- *Rising Strong,* by Brené Brown

- *Start with Why: How Great Leaders Inspire Everyone to Take Action,* by Simon Sinek

- *Strategy for YOU: Building a Bridge to the Life You Want,* by Rich Horwath

- *Thank You for Firing Me: How to Catch the Next Wave of Success After You Lose Your Job,* by Kitty Martini & Candice Reed

- *The Answer: Grow Any Business, Achieve Financial Freedom, and Live an Extraordinary Life,* by John Assaraf and Murray Smith

- *The Case for Hope: Looking Ahead With Confidence and Courage,* by Lee Strobel

- *The Complete Guide to Recovery from Job Loss: Get Your Life Back on Track with this Simple Guide,* by Lee Stewart

- *The Compound Effect,* by Darren Hardy

- *The Gift of Job Loss: A Practical Guide to Realizing the Most Rewarding Time of Your Life,* by Michael Froehls

- *The Gifts of Imperfection: Let Go of Who You Think You're Supposed to Be and Embrace Who You Are,* by Brene Brown

- *The How of Wow!* by John J. Murphy

- *The Job Loss Recovery Guide: A Proven Program for Getting Back to Work—Fast!,* by Lynn Joseph

- *The Job-Loss Recovery Program Guide: The Ultimate Visualization System for Landing a Great Job Now,* by Lynn Joseph

- *The Power of I Am: Two Words That Will Change Your Life Today,* by Joel Osteen

- *The Power to Shape Your Destiny: Seven Strategies for Massive Results,* by Tony Robbins

- *The Re-Examined Life: What is Possible After Job Loss?,* by Bill Van Steenis and Greg Smith

- *The Secret,* by Rhonda Byrne

- *The Upside to Job Loss: Finding Hope for the Future,* by Sheila M. Luck

- *Unlimited Power: The New Science of Personal Achievement,* by Tony Robbins

- *What I Know for Sure,* by Oprah Winfrey

- *When Hope Hurts,* by Carol E. Urton

- *Wishes Fulfilled: Mastering the Art of Manifesting,* by Wayne W. Dyer

- *You Are a Badass: How to Stop Doubting Your Greatness and Start Living an Awesome Life,* by Jen Sincero

- *You Can, You Will: 8 Undeniable Qualities of a Winner,* by Joel Osteen

- *You'll Land on Your Feet: How Anyone Can Survive and Thrive After Job Loss,* by Andre W. Renna

- *You're Fired!: Why Losing Your Job Might Be the Best Thing to Happen to You,* by Juergen Maslow

- *Your Erroneous Zones: Step-by-Step Advice for Escaping the Trap of Negative Thinking and Taking Control of Your Life,* by Wayne W. Dyer

- *Your Inner Awakening: The Work of Byron Katie—Four Questions That Will Transform Your Life,* by Byron Katie and Nightingale Conant

- *Zentrepreneur: Get Out of the Way and Lead, Create a Culture of Innovation and Fearlessness,* by John J. Murphy

A Course in Miracles, by Chris Cade and Marianne Williamson

A Course in Miracles is a complete self-study spiritual thought system. As a three-volume curriculum consisting of a Text, Workbook for Students, and Manual for Teachers, it teaches that the way to universal love and peace is through forgiving others. The Course thus focuses on the healing of relationships and making them holy.

Absolutely Abby, www.absolutelyabby.com

Job search and career enrichment secrets revealed by a Human Resources professional whose personal mission is to help everyone find his or her career passions.

COURAGEworks, with Brené Brown

Developed by Brené Brown, *COURAGEworks* is an online learning community that offers eCourses, workshops and interviews for anyone who is ready for braver living, loving and leading.

Finding Your Life's Purpose, by Eckhart Tolle

If you've been searching for your true purpose in life, Eckhart Tolle has some straightforward advice: Stop struggling. For the primary purpose of every human being is simply to be: fully engaged in this moment and aligned with the natural flow of reality itself.

On *Finding Your Life's Purpose*, the best-selling author of *A New*

Earth invites you to discover the twofold intention of our human incarnation: to free yourself from the prison of "thought-based reality," and to express in your own way the grand vision that universal consciousness has for your life.

Having It All; Achieving Your Life's Goals & Dreams, by John Assaraf

No matter what you want in your life, *Having It All* will take you from where you are to where you want to be. Entrepreneur John Assaraf started with nothing and went on to create a multimillion-dollar empire and achieve the life of his dreams, earning himself the nickname "The Street Kid." Now he shares the best of what he's learned so you, too, can create the life of your dreams. *Having It All* contains practical exercises and powerful lessons to help you achieve greater happiness and long-lasting success.

Living With the Law of Attraction, with Katherine Hurst

We are all a product of our thoughts. It is our own thoughts and energies that are continually creating the very life around us; learn how to become more deliberate and selective of your thoughts and emotions, and your life can become yours to create to your exact liking.

Living Your Best Year Ever, by Darren Hardy

Living Your Best Year Ever outlines the specific plan that Darren developed for himself, synthesizing hundreds of books, seminars, trials, errors and victories into the best and proven strategies on how to design, execute, stick to and achieve big goals.

MindShift: The Ultimate Success Course, by Steve Chandler

Ready for the world's most joyful challenge? The human system wants challenges. It was designed for challenges. It does not simply want comfort. The mind thinks it only wants comfort because it sees so many advertisements that sell comfort as the ultimate good thing. So it tries to comfort itself. It avoids challenge. But challenge is where the joy is. And MIND-shifting is the ultimate challenge.

NeuroGym, by John Assaraf

The latest scientific findings establish that you can change your life by changing your brain. For many years, scientists believed that your brain was a static, hard-wired organ—but the study of neuroplasticity has proven otherwise. Your brain is forming new connections and growing new brain cells every day. A study published in *Clinical Psychology Review* suggests that when you practice a variety of specific brain-related activities you have the ability to transform your health, finances, career and relationships. *NeuroGym* uses the latest brain science to help you achieve positive, lasting change—creating the life of your dreams.

Foundations for Success, with Jim Rohn

SUCCESS has spent the last year gathering all the courses, lessons and teachings from Mentor to the Masters Jim Rohn out of the archives and put them all together into this 10-module online training. You will get hours of video, days of audio and years of experience. Every lesson includes brand-new exclusive material from the Modern Masters including Tony Robbins, Brian Tracy, Darren Hardy, John C. Maxwell and more as they introduce you to the message from their perspective; as you dive in and learn from Jim Rohn.

Success Principles, with Jack Canfield

This book teaches how to increase your confidence, tackle daily challenges, live with passion and purpose and realize all your ambitions. Not merely a collection of good ideas, this book spells out the 67 timeless principles and practices used by the world's most successful men and women—proven principles and strategies that can be adapted for your own life, whether you want to be the best salesperson in your company, become a leading architect, score top grades in school, lose weight, buy your dream home, make millions or just get back in the job market.

COACHING

iPEC—Professional Excellence in Coaching

One of the largest ICF-accredited coach training schools in the world, iPEC has a proven track record of success—helping over 7,000 graduates launch careers as Certified Professional Coaches.

iPEC's mission is to help students have the greatest impact on the lives of others—by awakening their own passion, purpose and potential. Their personal-development systems and growth programs create leadership from the inside out helping students uncover their innate abilities and learn to leverage their strengths to effect change in others.

For more information on iPEC, go to www.ipeccoaching.com.

NATIONAL PROFESSIONAL ORGANIZATIONS

Society for Human Resources Management

Founded in 1948, the Society for Human Resource Management (SHRM) is the world's largest HR membership organization devoted to human resource management. Representing more than 275,000 members in over 160 countries, the society is the leading provider of resources to serve the needs of HR professionals and advance the professional practice of human resource management. SHRM has more than 575 affiliated chapters within the United States.

Ready to Work

In his 2014 State of the Union Address, President Obama announced that he was asking Vice President Biden to lead a review of federal training programs in order to identify and implement steps to make these programs more "job-driven": more responsive to the needs of employers and more effective in training and placing ready-to-work Americans.

Across the country, federal Ready to Work job training programs help hardworking Americans find good jobs and careers, help employers recruit and hire the workers they need to compete and help American communities build the workforces they need to attract business investments, and create jobs.

The overarching goal of these programs is to continue to grow the economy, expand opportunity and widen the pathway to the middle class for American workers.

In addition to all of these amazing resources, every state has its own programs, initiatives, organizations and businesses dedicated to helping individuals in transition who are between their "next wave of success." I would encourage everyone to do a Google search for a list of the resources available in your local area.

In my home state of New Jersey, here are just a few:

STATE SPECIFIC

New Start Career Network

While the job market in New Jersey is improving, more than 41 percent of the state's job seekers—more than 125,000 individuals—have been jobless for more than six months, giving New Jersey the second highest long-term unemployment rate in the nation. Additionally, thousands more have given up and dropped out of the labor force. Adding to the problem is the fact that the public workforce system offers few services targeted to the needs of the long-term unemployed, the reluctance of many employers to hire the long-term unemployed, and the difficulty job seekers face in finding reliable and unbiased information and advice.

To help long-term unemployed New Jerseyans, particularly those age 45 and older, obtain jobs, the Heldrich Center, with major support from the Philip and Tammy Murphy Family Foundation and other corporations and foundations, is launching the New Start Career Network (NSCN). NSCN is a multiyear effort involving employers, nonprofit organizations and Rutgers University to serve job seekers through web-based advising and information resources and personalized coaching. All services are provided free of charge to individuals who meet the program's basic criteria. Available services include:

- Information and advice about the labor market, careers, education and training.

- Counseling through peer-support networks and job clubs and via a volunteer job counseling corps of professionals and NSCN alumni.

- Incentives that encourage employers to provide trial employment opportunities and on-the-job training for long-term unemployed job seekers.

- Commitments from employers to reform hiring practices, building upon initiatives undertaken by the White House and AARP.

- Access and referral to a broad array of services, including education, training, mental health counseling and financial advising.

Society for Human Resources Management: Garden State Council

The Garden State Council (GSC) SHRM Workforce Readiness team is committed to establishing strategic reciprocal alliances with organizations and causes throughout the state that are dedicated to making a positive impact in all areas of workforce readiness. It is our goal to be recognized by businesses, education institutions and government bodies, as partners, collaborators, advocates and leaders in this field.

Ready to Work: New Jersey (RTWNJ)

The Ready to Work New Jersey program helps long-term unemployed people (six months or longer) get back to work quickly. Eligible registered candidates receive services to help them be more marketable during their job searches and offers job leads through one of the major job board providers. The program offers workshop training in résumé writing, interviewing skill sand use of social media for networking. RTWNJ also offers a personal assessment tool so candidates can determine their professional strengths and weaknesses and, once recognized, help improve key areas through training. RTWNJ also offers counseling services to candidates to discuss job search strategies and additional occupational training opportunities they may need to be competitive with other job seekers. Employers can also benefit through on-the-job salary reimbursement for the first six months or $10,000, whichever comes first, whenever a candidate is placed. The program is in place until October 2018.

ACKNOWLEDGMENTS

First and foremost, I give thanks to my source of all things, my Creator and Heavenly Father who has blessed my life in countless ways. I owe my life to You.

Thank you, from the bottom of my heart, to all who contributed and granted permission to publish their stories in this book. You selflessly shared your trials, tribulations and triumphs in the *hope* that it would someday inspire or help someone who is currently struggling. I am, and I'm certain our readers will be, in awe of the insights, courage, strength, resilience and perseverance that brought you each to a place of peace and fulfillment. May your kindness and generosity come back to you a million times over.

Once again I must acknowledge and thank the loves, light and energy of my life: my parents, brother and children. You have been by my side, supporting, loving and believing in me for as long as I can remember. There are no words to express just how grateful I am and how much I love you with all my heart and soul.

Thank you, my dear friend, colleague and book coach, Michelle Tillis Lederman of Executive Essentials. My little firecracker—you've been my biggest supporter and advocate from day one. Very likely, without your encouragement, guidance and direction, this book might never have seen the light of day. Thank you for your selflessness and, most importantly, your friendship.

> For information on Michelle's services and a free chapter from her book *The 11 Laws of Likability*, go to www.executiveessentials.org.

My dear friend and mindfulness guru, Julie Murphy, thank you for being my sounding board whenever I needed it. Thank you for your coaching, guidance and editorial contributions. Most importantly, thank you to Jocelyn Seals for inviting me to your mindfulness workshop. It really educated and turned me on to achieving a mindfulness practice in my life, a priceless gift. For information on how to transform how you show up in the world, go to www.oakwoodleadership.com.

Thank you to my first real life coach, Joanne Bobes, who asked me one of the most thought-provoking questions. Joanne, your extraordinary coaching skills, support and friendship paved the way to a whole new vision for my life. You're an inspiration and role model.

My incredible book production team, thanks to Michelle for all the referrals:

- Janica Smith, of PublishingSmith, for making my dream come to life through your management of the project, holding my hand and helping me stay on track. For information on Janica's publishing services, go to www.PublishingSmith.com.

- Meeghan Truelove, my extraordinary editor, thank you for your patience and creativity. You are absolutely brilliant, and I just love what we were able to create together.

- Fred Pesce of Vertigo Media Group, you designed my amazing cover with very little vision or direction. It was as if you could read my mind. I love it so much. Thank you for your talent and your friendship. To contact Fred and learn about his services, go to www.VertigoMediaGrp.com.

Throughout my journey, I do believe several "angels" were sent to help guide my way. These beautiful, kind, like-minded souls are still in my life today, and their friendship means the world to me. In no particular order:

Heather Clarke-Peckerman, Dena Moscola, Dean Hoffman, Tammy (Mama Bear) Clarke, Jocelyn Seals, Tara Seager, Julie Murphy, Debbie Gencarelli, Michelle Tillis Lederman, Lydia Gennace, Natasha Sullivan, Leisa Suchan, Elle Demetriou, Ivy Olivé, Kristen Swarcheck, Rosh Rupani—ladies and gentleman you are my soul sisters and brothers, my biggest fans and supporters. You light my flame every time it starts to dim, and I will forever be thankful for you in my life.

ABOUT THE AUTHOR

After 24 years of working at the same financial services corporation, Christina DeOliveira came into work one morning only to discover her position was being eliminated due to budget cuts. Coming on the heels of several traumatic and heartbreaking family tragedies, Christina struggled to find her equilibrium— until she finally found the courage to confront her future and find a rich new professional life she never dreamed was possible. Thus came the inspiration to write *The JOY of Losing Your Job*, in which Christina shares not only her own inspiring story, but those of others who experienced the same midlife renaissance after first being brutally terminated by a longtime employer.

In addition to authoring *The JOY of Losing Your Job*, Christina DeOliveira is the founder and principal consultant of Performance Continuum, a successful strategic management consultancy with expertise in human capital management, leadership development, creating high-performance cultures, team alignment and engagement, leadership coaching, and service excellence.

She is also the founder and president of David's Gift, a scholarship foundation dedicated to memorializing the life of her beloved brother, David, and to which proceeds from the sale of this book are donated.

Christina is grateful to be living her dream life and engaged in work that creates joy, happiness, inspiration and hope for herself and others. Her favorite pastime is enjoying the company of her cherished family and friends. She lives in New Jersey with her family.

For more information on Christina and her work, go to: www.performancecontinuum.com.

NOTES

NOTES

NOTES

NOTES

NOTES

NOTES